Paola Giovetti

ROBERTO ASSAGIOLI

The Life and Work
of the
Founder of Psychosynthesis

Revised Edition
with a Foreword by Sergio Guarino

*Translated and Edited with Additional Notes
by
Jan Kuniholm*

Kentaur Publishing

Copyright © 1995/2024 by Edizioni Mediterranee via Flaminia 109 – 00196 Roma
www.edizionimediterranee.net

This Edition and English Translation Copyright © Kentaur Publishing 2024

All Rights Reserved. No part of this publication may be reproduced, distributed, utilized or transited in any form or by any means, including photocopying, recording, or other electronic or mechanical methods, or by any information storage or retrieval system, without prior written permission of Kentaur Publishing, except in the case of brief quotations embodied in reviews and certain non-commercial uses.

Cover Photo Courtesy of Isabelle Clotilde Küng
Interior Photos courtesy of Edizioni Mediterranee
Front Cover Design by Byhaugereitz.dk
Interior Book Design by Simona Meloni

Published by Kentaur Publishing
Oslo, Norway
www.kennethsorensen.dk
Mail: ks@kennethsorensen.dk

EAN: 9788269382204
ISBN: 978-82-693822-0-4

CONTENTS

Translator's Note v
Foreword to the 2024 Edition by Sergio Guarino vii
Introduction xi
Preface xiii
Life and Work of Roberto Assagioli 1
Brief Note to the Reader 3
1) The Formative Years 5
Childhood and Early Youth 5
    The University Years 9
    Psychagogy 18
    The Sexual Question 20
    The Medical Degree 24
    Relations with C.G. Jung 25
    Psiche 28
2) Years of Maturity 43
    World War I. Marriage and Move to Rome 43
    The Birth of Psychosynthesis 44
    Religion, Esotericism and Eastern Spirituality 48
    The Institute of Culture and Psychic Therapy 54
    The Family 59
    The Second World War. Freedom in Jail 64
    The Resumption of Work 70
    Progressive Judaism 74
    The Death of Ilario 78
    Consolidation of the Work 82
3) Roberto Assagioli Up Close 87
Interviews with Luisa Ferrari, Donatella Ciapetti Assagioli, Amedeo Rotondi, Sergio Bernardi, Sergio Bartoli, Ferruccio Antonelli, Teresa D'Amico, Piero Ferrucci, Bruno Caldironi, Massimo Rosselli, Andrea Bocconi, Matilde Santandrea, Vittorio Arzilla, Ada Cini, Susanne Nouvion, Peter De Roche Coppens

4) The Last Years. "Liberation" 135
   The Fruitful Time of Old Age 135
   Roberto Assagioli Alone 138
   Liberation 141
5) Smiling Wisdom 143
6) Roberto Assagioli and Borderline Issues 161
7) Biopsychosynthesis 163

Appendix: Meditation and Contemplation, by Roberto Assagioli 173
The Assagioli Archives 183

Selected Bibliography 181

Psychosynthesis in the World 185

Translator's Note

It is a pleasure to bring a work about Roberto Assagioli to English-speaking readers, whose interest in his writing a few years ago could be satisfied by only a handful of pamphlets published by the Psychosynthesis Research Foundation, the two major books he published in English, and one other book that had been compiled after his death and translated twice. Recently my colleague Catherine Ann Lombard has rendered a wonderful service to the psychosynthesis community by translating *Freedom in Jail* and *Creating Harmony in Life*, and these are important additions to the psychosynthesis literature in English.

Those of us of have done a little research have felt an increasing lack, because some essential aspects of psychosynthesis are not presented thoroughly in those published works, or in other works by English-speaking authors who have not had access to the vast store of Assagioli's writings in other languages, so some important other features of Assagioli's teaching seemed to missing from them.

English-speaking readers, teachers, and practitioners of psychosynthesis have had no idea what they have been missing, because the material has been available only in the Assagioli Archives in Italian and sometimes French or German! I have been working with Kenneth Sörensen and Kentaur Publishing for a few years now, and we have translated nearly 200 of Assagioli's talks, lectures, and papers that until now have been available only in Italian. English-speaking readers can access them online at https://kennethsorensen.dk/en/.

Now with the translation and publication of this fine book by Paola Giovetti, originally published in 1995, we have another resource in learning about Roberto Assagioli and Psychosynthesis. This book fills in a gap in our learning in two important ways: it tells us more about Roberto the man, and it also provides insights into him and his work by some of his last students.

In this edition I have added notes that clarify the author's original notes and that give information about topics in the text that may be unfamiliar to English-speaking readers. I have distinguished the original author's notes from my additions by putting my additional notes *in italics* and identifying my additions with —*Ed*. In some cases I have felt the need to alert the reader that I am making an interpolation of the original text, usually for the benefit of non-Italian speakers, and on these occasions my interpolations are indicated by text [in brackets].

I am grateful to the author for her work and hope that this translation can do justice to the original. Any defects or shortcomings here are mine, not hers. I am grateful to Bonney Kuniholm and Audrey McMorrow for assistance with copy editing and proofreading, and to Kenneth Sörensen for making this all possible.

—Cheshire, Massachusetts, September 2024

Jan Kuniholm (b. Massachusetts, 1948) has been personally involved with Psychosynthesis since 2002, when he began professional training at The Synthesis Center in Amherst, MA. Since that time he served the Association for the Advancement of Psychosynthesis (AAP) in many capacities, including organizing conferences and collecting archival material, and as Co-Chair of its Steering Committee. He was the founder and editor of the online magazine *Psychosynthesis Quarterly*. He has edited and published several books connected with Psychosynthesis, including *Sharing Wellness: Psychosynthesis for Helping People: Theory and Applications*, a collection of classic articles; and *Psychosynthesis of the Couple: Men and Women in Relationships*, by Roberto Assagioli, MD, a synthetic essay he translated and created from many of Assagioli's writings on this topic. Since 2018 he has focused on translating essays, talks and other writings of Roberto Assagioli from Italian into English, and has completed the translations of over 175 of these documents, many of which are posted online at https://kennethsorensen.dk/en/. He and his wife Bonney are currently working on writing a new book focusing on men and women in couples relationships. They live in Cheshire, Massachusetts.

Foreword to the 2024 Edition
Sergio Guarino

In early 1974, Eugene Smith, an American physician from Boston, asked Roberto Assagioli to dictate his memoirs. Assagioli agreed, and Smith began recording the Venetian psychiatrist's recollections in April of that year. Unfortunately, Assagioli died the following August, and his memoirs remained limited to a few youthful recollections. In the later years of his life the founder of psychosynthesis had achieved a certain fame, and there were several students, both from Italy and abroad, who wanted to learn his method.

In Assagioli's vision, man possesses the ability to transcend and objectify himself, and this enables him to be able to become his own educator. In his article, "Per una moderna psicagogia," ["For a Modern Psychagogy"] which appeared on Feb. 25, 1909 in Prezzolini's journal *La Voce*, Assagioli, who was only twenty-one years old, wrote,

> (It is an error) not to consider the child as the future person, and to interrupt one's [educational] activity at the very age when it would begin to be truly fruitful. Just when the youngster is most capable of being educated, because on the one hand he has not yet lost the great flexibility of childhood, and on the other hand, his more mature mind and his greater capacity for attention, his greater energy makes him able to take advantage much more than the child of every help and advice — just then, modern education can give him nothing but a flood of knowledge and impose on him the obligation to be 'obedient, composed and diligent!'

"Psychagogy, on the other hand," Assagioli continues,

> says that since a person is never something definite, static, or complete, but is in continuous formation, education must continue throughout life: that the same psychological laws which regulate the psychic life of the child also regulate that of the adult, and that therefore the same methods which serve for the education of the one serve, with appropriate adjustments, for the education of the other.

Already evident in this article is the concept of lifelong education and the profound understanding of how fundamental it is to teach self-cultivation throughout one's life, as he will do for himself. I would say that these words are the seed of psychosynthesis itself: in them the father of our school already combines neo-Platonism in a perfect synthesis with the ideas of phenomenology and existentialism, the most advanced philosophy of his time.

These three philosophical roots, neo-Platonism, existentialism and phenomenology, together with his interests in theosophy and Hindu culture, would soon lead him to critique and go beyond the naturalistic conceptions in Freud's psychoanalysis, from which he distanced himself. All this in order to arrive at a psychology that centers on not simply the human being, but his essence, and on the educational and therapeutic value of the recognition of this essential nature, which is awareness and also the will — a will with a central role, precisely because it is understood as a responsive, dynamic aspect of consciousness itself.

This is what Assagioli teaches us: to bring attention to this invisible dimension and to discover that we are this invisible dimension, this "other" nature: an original nature totally different from merely phenomenal reality.

This is man's consciousness, a *noumenal* reality, the part of his own soul that is present in the world. In his vision, the universe tends toward synthesis, which for Assagioli is synonymous with evolution, and man's consciousness is the preeminent protagonist through which this synthesis can proceed and take place. The work of man is therefore to realize this synthesis first of all within himself, recognizing and knowing from this inner dimension how to distinguish what is central from what is peripheral, the essential from the external, the profound from the superficial.

For Assagioli, educating really corresponds to an act of "drawing out," as the very etymology of the word says — something that cannot be conceived by the current positivist and mechanistic paradigm that still prevails throughout the Western world and, perhaps, we could say by now, universally. That paradigm is still slow to recognize the child's natural and innate heritage of inner gifts, and continues to consider that values are something that can only be bestowed from the outside.

Assagioli, on the other hand, knows well that the higher values are already in the child and the task of education is only to evoke them; education that is imposed can easily lead to rejection, harming what could and should be a spontaneous, natural awareness.

Picasso said, "*Every child is creative; the real challenge is to remain that way while growing up.*" We adults, on the other hand, often tend to suppress this creativity in our children, because we want them to be quiet, silent and obedient. Assagioli is fully aware that good pedagogy should never be forced; he knows well that coercion ends up ruining the spontaneous creativity of the child; that only freedom will allow the creativity of the future man, avoiding conformism but above all allowing him to be truly useful to society, by means of a thinking that can see what is new and undertake it. And all this becomes even more important today in a world that is about to delegate all repetitive work to mechanical robots.

We now know that man's work in the immediate future will increasingly rely on his creative capacity and ability to renew himself professionally. Education can continue in the adult with self-education, and in particular with the technique of creating an external unifying center, a creation that makes use of the perception of one's own center to intuit and bring into manifestation a new personality that allows one to draw closer to one's self. This involves intuiting how to better perceive and express realistically *what we can be*, imagining it as our ideal model and undertaking a practice to realize it, to bring into manifestation in a practical way — our new way of being, a personality that we feel is most like us, that allows us to express ourselves better. Of course, this presupposes the study and knowledge of the various aspects and mechanisms of the human psyche, enabling clarity about one's inner world and requiring outside help initially. But the mature individual who, with help, has been able to identify with his own "I" or self, with his own consciousness, can achieve an integration and synthesis of the various aspects that make up his personality through self-observation. He can discover his own will as a dynamic aspect of his consciousness and work to bring his own latent capacities into manifestation, to bring himself into expression.

For Assagioli, to express oneself better is to get closer to one's Self, meaning the unconscious, potential "I" of which the phenomenal "I" or self we express in everyday life is only a reflection. It is in self-expression that man is able to give meaning to his life, the meaning he seeks and which so often seems to elude him. "Bringing oneself into expression" means becoming more and more one's self, and presupposes a work of self-transcendence that eventually brings us closer to an identification with life itself and with humanity, allowing us to overcome the suffocating and illusory coincidence of the "I" with our own personality. As with Viktor Frankl, for Assagioli man truly becomes himself when he overcomes and forgets himself.

Paola Giovetti had the important merit of writing the first real biography of this great Italian, who has been known and admired more abroad than in Italy. This book was published by Edizioni Mediterranee in 1995 and is now being reissued with additional writings by Roberto Assagioli, some additions by the author, and this brief foreword of mine. Within it you will find descriptions of all the stages of the life of Assagioli, who never stopped working on himself, carrying out his own psychosynthesis. My teacher, Sergio Bartoli, who was a direct disciple of Assagioli (whose interview you will find along with others in this beautifully constructed book) told me one day that he asked his teacher what had been the period of his life when he had achieved the best results in his own personal evolution. Assagioli answered him that this was happening right then: he was 86 years old, only a few months away from his death.

Sergio Guarino (b. Catania, 1957) has a degree in Pharmacy from the University of Catania. Since 2020 he has been president of the Institute of Psychosynthesis founded by Roberto Assagioli. He trained in Gestalt Psychology and Psychosynthesis, and has led groups for self-knowledge and personal evolution since 1988. His teacher was psychotherapist Sergio Bartoli, a direct student of Assagioli. From 2010 to 2021 he was Director of the Catania Center for Psychosynthesis, and is the Founder and Coordinator of the Study & Research Group of the Catania Center for Psychosynthesis. He is a trainer at the Institute and Editor-in-Chief of its Scientific Committee, and Editor of the journal *Psychosynthesis*, in which he has published numerous articles. He has been an organizer and speaker at several national and international conferences. He is the author of the books *Approdi Invisibili* [*Invisible Landing*] (2016), *La vita Ispirata* [*The Inspired Life*] (2022), published by Euno Editions, of which he is also editor and for which he created the series of essays, "The Rose and the Key." Together with Mauro Ventola, he published *L'Esperienza Transpersonale - Dall'essere all'esserci: fenomenologia dell'essere nell'esistenza* [*The Transpersonal Experience - From Being to Being: Phenomenology of Being in Existence*] (2021) for ITI Editions.

INTRODUCTION
In Roberto Assagioli's Study

*A*nyone who wants to try to get to know Roberto Assagioli should spend at least a few hours in his study: a small room with a window overlooking the Fiesole hillside, on the second floor of the little villa at Via San Domenico No. 16 in Florence. This was his home and now houses the Institute of Psychosynthesis.

Everything in this study remains as it was when Assagioli was alive: the desk on which small familiar objects are neatly arranged — pencils, pens, paper, the ink dryer, the letter opener, a desk clock, a model ship with sails — and a fresh rose which is never missing, as in his own time. There is also a framed reproduction of a high mountain with a white snowy peak. The rose and the mountain are two important symbols in psychosynthesis, expressing the opening of the potential of Humanity and the upward tension — Assagioli evidently wanted to have them always present.

In front, on a cabinet, there are two cards with the evocative words, "serenity," and "patience," perhaps those recently chosen by Assagioli.

The walls of the study are covered with the books he consulted daily: The Bhagavad-Gita, Plotinus, writings on Zen, meditation and Christian mysticism, The Bible, Jewish Studies; also C. G. Jung, clinical texts, and the Encyclopedia Britannica. The multilingualism is striking: the books are in many languages and Assagioli knew many perfectly.

The wall is entirely occupied by the archive: a vast store of material divided by themes: handwritten notes (typewritten ones are rare) not yet fully studied; thoughts, insights, cues, ideas . . . The breadth of Assagioli's thought can especially be appreciated here.

In Roberto Assagioli's small, simple study, the noise of the street is muffled, and you can isolate yourself and allow yourself to be completely immersed in the atmosphere that you breathe in there, to be pervaded by it. Sitting at his desk in his swivel armchair, I see before me on the wall portraits of Assagioli himself, his wife Nella, and his beloved son Ilario, who died at the age of 28. I hold in my hands the sheets written in his own hand, in his typical ornate but confident handwriting. I read them slowly and copy some: wonderful little drops of wisdom, goodness, harmony, humor.

Hours go by without my noticing. Evening falls on the Fiesole hill, and as the sky grows dark and the first star appears, I open the folder with the words "Grandeur of the Universe." In many small sheets Roberto Assagioli expressed his amazement and admiration for the *boundless starry skies, for the infinite universe that seemed him to have the ability to create and maintain an attitude he cared so much about, and which is so difficult to make one's own: the sense of right proportion.*

On one of the sheets I read an anecdote that Assagioli particularly liked that he had taken from The Book of Naturalists by W. Beebe. This scientist, who was a friend of Theodore Roosevelt, used to spend many evenings in the company of the then President of the United States, and at one point they would go out to admire the starry sky. When the two friends were able to spot the faint Andromeda nebula, Beebe would say, "That is the spiral nebula Andromeda. It is as large as our Milky Way. It is one of a hundred million galaxies. It consists of one hundred billion suns, each larger than our sun." At this point Roosevelt interrupted him and said, smiling, "Now I think we are small enough. Let's go to bed!"[1]

I close the file and put it on the shelf and, after a last look at the evening light on the hill, I tiptoe out of the small study, in which the wise and smiling old gentleman continues to live; as if he is not gone, but always there, and invites us still to keep the right sense of proportion and to look to the highest.

Dear Maestro, I feel very small, but I will try to tell your story anyway. With the pen, but also with the heart.[2]

— P.G.

---

[1] Taken from the account in English by Beebe in Assagioli Archive Doc. #12490. —Tr.

[2] I would like to express my gratitude to the Institute of Psychosynthesis in Florence, which gave me permission to access Roberto Assagioli's study and to study the archive material.

PREFACE
"An Ancient Soul..."

In 1979, five years after the death of Roberto Assagioli, psychologist and psychoanalyst Sebastiano A. Tilli, a friend of the founder of psychosynthesis who was an excellent connoisseur of his work and a collaborator at the Institute of Psychosynthesis in Florence, observed in his book *Concetti della psicologia umanistica di Roberto Assagioli* [*Concepts of the Humanistic Psychology of Roberto Assagioli*][3] that it was still difficult to explain and "place" Assagioli with confidence, even with the growing enthusiasm that psychosynthesis aroused.

Today, after several years, we are faced with a similar situation, although some fundamental works by Assagioli have been published[4] and interest in the movement inspired by him is constantly growing.

In its "apparent simplicity" (S.A. Tilli's words), Assagioli's work is extremely complex and offers an infinite number of ideas, stimuli and suggestions that embrace the whole biopsychic and spiritual sphere of man. It is a very broad vision — perhaps the largest, richest, healthiest and most dynamic that has been formulated so far. This is a conception that is still waiting to be fully discovered and that can truly help man to achieve inner growth, to develop his potential, to realize himself in a positive and creative way, to become a person who is attentive to the here and now, but also firmly anchored in the transcendent dimension.

In addition to psychiatric and psychotherapeutic issues, Assagioli also dealt with interpersonal, family, social and group problems. He presented an educational psychology in the broadest sense of the term and addressed its humanistic and transpersonal aspects, emphasizing the need — innate in every human being — for spiritual elevation, for growth and evolution. He also presented practical and technical exercises to achieve these goals.

---

[3] Published by the Institute of Psychosynthesis in Florence, 1980.

[4] *L'atto di volontà*, 1977, and *Lo sviluppo transpersonale*, 1988, both published by Astrolabe, Rome. The The Act of Will *was published first in English by Turnstone Press in 1974 and* Transpersonal Development *was published in English translation in 2007 by Inner Way Productions.* —Ed.

Highly cultivated and knowledgeable in many languages, Assagioli was also interested in literature and philosophy, esotericism, parapsychology and Eastern spirituality. As one who knew the human soul and the multiple tendencies and conflicts that live within it, Assagioli pointed toward the possible harmonization of these elements, urging man to become, to use Friedrich Nietzsche's words, "what he actually is."

His psychosynthesis indicates the way to synthesis, to unity — a difficult way: "It is a conquest," says Assagioli. "It is the highest reward of a long labor, a tireless work, but one that is magnificent, varied, fascinating, and enriching for us and for others, even before it is ever completed."[5]

Wise, modest, tolerant, loving, joyful, serene despite his many problems and pains, Roberto Assagioli provided ideas and stimuli and personally participated in two great revolutions in psychology: first, the psychoanalysis of Freud, of which he was the first popularizer in Italy; then humanistic and transpersonal psychology.

He died leaving a seemingly infinite amount of material, handwritten notes, ideas, newly sketched programs and suggestions. His students and successors have been collating, studying and developing this material, highlighting their potential: an authentic message addressed to people of today and tomorrow.

With this book, which is not addressed so much to professionals as to all those who care about their mental and spiritual health and want to grow inwardly, I set out to reconstruct, albeit broadly, a biography of Roberto Assagioli, and to offer an introduction to his psychology. I don't know whether I have managed to do justice to the vastness and loftiness of the wisdom of this authentic initiate of our time ("an ancient soul" as he was called by Dr. Sergio Bartoli — one of the people who was closest to him in the last twenty years of life), who is today perhaps more appreciated abroad than in Italy. I can say, however, that I approached this work with love, humility and a spirit of service, and I was amply rewarded for it. By "taking care of" Roberto Assagioli for a long time, I have learned many things and I myself have received genuine help from his "smiling wisdom."

I thank all those who willingly collaborated in my research: without them, this work would not have been possible.

---

[5] Roberto Assagioli, *Psychosynthesis, Harmony of Life,* Mediterranean Editions, Rome, 1971, p. 22. Translation of this passage is by Catherine Ann Lombard in *Creating Harmony in Life,* Istituto di Psicosintesi 2022, p. 15. —*Ed.*

LIFE AND WORK
OF
ROBERTO ASSAGIOLI

BRIEF NOTE FOR THE READER

Reconstructing the life of Roberto Assagioli has not been easy: he himself was always very reserved about his private life, unlike C.G. Jung, who in the last years of his life collaborated with Aniela Jaffè to write the famous *Memories, Dreams, Reflections*, revealing a great deal about himself. Sigmund Freud, for his part, left various autobiographical writings, such as his *Autobiographical Study* and certain paragraphs in *The Psychopathology of Daily Life*. He also had biographers who knew and followed him for a long time, such as Ernest Jones, author of the famous *Life and Work of Sigmund Freud,* and himself a psychoanalyst.

Assagioli did not write memoirs, but only an extremely thin profile (two typewritten folders available at the Florence Institute), and left his students the moral obligation for confidentiality. To this state of affairs was added the destruction of material that was certainly of great interest: two fires, apparently due to anti-Semitic persecutions (Assagioli was Jewish); one in the house in Rome where he lived before the Second World War; the other at his summer residence in Tuscany, which reduced part of the archive to ashes.

In Assagioli's biography there are years of which almost nothing is known and others with little more. However, some writings were salvaged and it was possible to consult them; an excellent work of research and documentation related to Assagioli's formative years was carried out by Alessandro Berti of Florence;[6] and direct testimonials from people who were in contact with the founder of psychosynthesis made it possible to fill in certain gaps while respecting the need for discretion.

Roberto Assagioli, however, did not give much importance to his personal affairs, and Assagioli the man is found above all in his writings: what he cared about above all was to leave an idea, a model of life, naturally in line with his psychosynthetic conception.

---

[6] The essay by A. Berti began as a thesis and was published with the title: *Roberto Assagioli. The Formative Years*, by the Institute of Psychosynthesis of Florence, in 1987. A book edited by Alessandro Berti was also very useful: *Roberto Assagioli 1888-1988:* a photographic documentation of the fundamental aspects of cultural, social, emotional and work life, enriched with documents and notes, which appeared on the centenary of his birth, published by Psychosynthesis Study Center of Florence.

Surprisingly, in 2018 a "fragment of an autobiography" begun and recorded by Boston physician Eugene Smith, but sadly soon discontinued due to Assagioli's death, was made public through publication by the Institute of Psychosynthesis in Florence. Smith visited Assagioli and proposed that he write his biography, a proposal that was accepted in the hope that it would interest the public and invite them to read his books and learn more about his work. The two met in April 1974 and then the following August, but Assagioli fell ill with the flu, then succumbed to pneumonia, and within days this led to his death on August 23.

Eugene Smith transcribed the interviews, then interviewed some people who had known the creator of psychosynthesis. Assagioli's intention was to make a book of it all, but he did not live long enough to carry out his project. The material remained forgotten for several years until Tom Yeomans, a student of Assagioli, obtained permission from Eugene Smith's family to publish something, and he asked the Institute of Psychosynthesis if they would be willing to work on it. The answer was positive, and so it was done, leaving Assagioli's talks as they were, word for word, without filter or commentary. The text appeared in 2019 under the title *Roberto Assagioli In His Own Words - Fragments of an Autobiography*, recorded by Eugene Smith, edited by Gianni Dattilo, Piero Ferrucci, and Vivien Reid Ferrucci, and was published by Edizioni Istituto di Psicosintesi, Florence. I will draw excerpts from it to supplement the information available previously.

Thus was born this biography, for which I met and interviewed Assagioli's last students, whom I thank for their willingness and generosity to cooperate. I also interviewed relatives, family friends, and tenants, each of whom added something personal and valuable to the information I had. The biography of the Master will always be interwoven with the "red thread" of his psychosynthesis and the description of the many cultural and thought movements in which he was interested.

Assagioli himself suggested that his students and patients read biographies of "ideal" characters to refer to in order to grow: I hope that reading the life events and above all the evolution of the thought of the founder of psychosynthesis can now be a stimulus for those who are searching.

CHAPTER 1
THE FORMATIVE YEARS

Every one of us can and must fashion from the living material of his personality, whether it be silver, marble or gold, an object of beauty through which he can adequately manifest his Transpersonal Self.
— (R. Assagioli, *Psychosynthesis Typology*, p. 16).[7]

CHILDHOOD AND EARLY YOUTH

Roberto Assagioli, whose original name was Roberto Marco Grego, was born in Venice on February 27, 1888 to Jewish parents. His mother, Elena Kaula, was from a Venetian family but was born in Egypt; his father Leone was an engineer from Verona.

Of his birth and early years Assagioli writes in his unfinished autobiography:[8]

> I was born in Venice, Italy, on the twenty-seventh of February in the year 1888, in the neighborhood of Cannaregio near the Ca'd'Oro, the golden palace on the Grand Canal.
>
> My birth was difficult. For a number of years I was fragile, and not strong. My father was ill, and when I was two years of age he died of tuberculosis. I was born with the right foot twisted — a clubfoot. The family doctor very ably straightened it when I was a few months old without an operation, without cutting, just by bending it gradually. But it remains a clubfoot to this day. At one time I had to wear metal braces in the shoe. The family doctor who corrected it took a great liking to me and some time later married my mother and adopted me, so from then on I called him "Father." Of my real father I remember almost nothing, since I was only two years old when he died. Assagioli is the name of my stepfather, while the name of my natural father was Grego.

---

[7] *This passage is taken from the English edition of* Psychosynthesis Typology *published by the Institute of Psychosynthesis, London, in 1983. —Ed.*

[8] *The passages from this unfinished biography are taken from the published English-language edition of 2019. —Tr.*

Dr. Alessandro Assagioli was a very loving father for Roberto. He devoted himself to the boy's education with great generosity, intelligence and love. Of his parents, Assagioli speaks in these terms:

> The influence of both my mother and father has been greatly significant. My mother was born of Italian parents, but in Egypt. After a few years her mother died, and her father, who was in trade, sent her to what was called a *collegio*, a woman's boarding school. There she studied intensely. She stayed in Egypt a long time — until she married. The professors were very good. She did mainly classical studies, foreign languages, French and English, and in the last year the professor, not knowing what else to teach her, taught her Greek. She was highly cultured and a voracious reader, a propensity which I have inherited.
>
> I am appreciative and very grateful to her because, although she loved me very much, she left me quite free. At that time, at the turn of the century, this was exceptional. She was not at all possessive in her affection. Also, she helped me in my studies. When I began to write, I dictated to her sometimes into the small hours of the morning. We were very close, but she always left me free.
>
> My father, that is, my stepfather, Dr. Alessandro Assagioli, was also exceptional in many ways. He was a medical doctor, highly intelligent, but in particular he was very intuitive. The diagnoses he sometimes made intuitively were amazing. He had a fine career. . .

The stimulating family environment along with his father's considerable economic resources ensured that Roberto was able to cultivate his wide-ranging interests. Indeed, from a very young age he frequented diverse circles, played various sports, and traveled.

Alessandro Assagioli was always willing to accommodate his son's desires. "He was in no way possessive," Roberto Assagioli continues to relate:

> At first he tried to orient me to an engineering career — civil engineering — which had been the profession of my original father. But I had neither liking nor talent for mathematics and drawing. One day I declared to him that I wanted to become a medical doctor . . . he helped me a lot, and he too left me free. It was extraordinary for the times that he had such an idea of freedom.

"Later," the autobiography continues, "something that touched me very much came to light."

Many years later my mother was speaking with friends, telling them how anxious she had been while I was on those trips:[9] but she had never let me know that, so as not to spoil my pleasure. I have been very fortunate with my parents.

There was a great emphasis in the family on foreign languages. Assagioli recounts:

It was my father's idea that I should be raised in three languages. So within the family we would speak one day Italian, one day French, and one day English. We did this from when I was three, so I learned each language like mother tongues. Then when I was eight years old they found a professor to teach me German . . .

He had such a mastery of English that he was able to write some of his most important works in this language, which were only translated into Italian at a later date: this is the case, for example, with *The Act of Will*.[10] Later he learned a little Russian, in preparation for a trip to that country; and then German, of which he had a knowledge that Sigmund Freud described as "impeccable." His perfect command of German allowed him later to attend, as we will see, the Burghölzli psychiatric hospital in Zurich, where he met C.G. Jung, and the psychoanalytic circles revolving around S. Freud. He had a personal relationship with Freud himself.

Assagioli continues:

My father also took good care of my health and encouraged me in sports. The first sport was swimming, for which Venice gave great opportunities. Very early he sent me alone to swim in the canal and also out into the expanse of the Lagoon. Then came rowing, both the Venetian way of rowing, standing up, as well as the usual way.

And here comes my first, let us call it spiritual experience, at the age of twelve. I was in a boat, far out, in a silent expanse of water. I let go of the

---

[9] *More about the trips is related below.* —Ed.

[10] *The Act of Will*, has been masterfully translated into Italian by Maria Luisa Girelli Macchia, Director of the Psychosynthesis Center in Rome and published by Astrolabio, Rome, 1977; she also edited the edition and publication of *Transpersonal Development*, published posthumously in 1988 by Astrolabio. *The first English edition of* The Act of Will *was published in Great Britain by Turnstone Press in 1974, and* Transpersonal Development *has been published in English by Inner Way Productions in Scotland in 2007.* —Ed.

oars and just looked at the peaceful scenery. Out of the sky came a phrase, "I want to be always present to myself." Of course, at that time I didn't realize the import, but I did know that it gave me a sense of joy. It was just a momentary episode, and then I came back to earth.

Roberto Assagioli's father also encouraged him to go hiking in the mountains, first along with him and then on his own, sometimes availing himself of a guide for more challenging trips. Assagioli always had a great love for the mountains and, in addition to trips, he also willingly undertook real climbs, with the great pleasure of reaching the summit.

Here is one of his comments:

What I have told you about mountain climbing gives sufficient reason on the personal level for my liking and my enthusiasm for it: the beauty of nature and the sense of power and the welcoming of dizziness and pain and all that. I had a sense of superiority when up there, thinking of the poor people down at the bottom of the valley just waking up after a night of dancing and drinking, with a bad tongue and a headache. But all that is at the personal level. Later I discovered the higher meaning, the symbolism of mountain climbing. It all ties in with Maslow's idea of peak and plateau experiences. A few years ago I gave a lecture on the symbolism of mountain climbing, which I transformed into an article.[11]

Some of the fundamental themes of Roberto Assagioli's thought thus have their spontaneous roots in early youth.

In Venice, Assagioli attended the *Liceo Foscarini*, graduating in 1904 with very high marks, when he was only 16. As Alessandro Berti rightly observes in his study, the Foscarini High School gave equal importance to classical and scientific studies, which allowed Assagioli to open himself in both directions and to develop his interest in science, literature and the philosophy that would be with him throughout his life.

At just 15 years of age, Roberto Assagioli began writing and publishing: two articles appeared in the *Giornale di Venezia* [Venice Journal] in 1903 which revealed his early social and cultural interests. The first concerns a student protest against

---

[11] Roberto Assagioli, "Psychological Mountain Climbing," *Corso di lezioni sulla Psicosintesi*, 1970, Lezione X, Istituto di Psicosintesi. *Also published by the Psychosynthesis Research Foundation as part of PRF Issue No .36, 1976.—Ed.*

the Ministry of Education: with great balance and maturity the young Roberto took a position in favor of those who conscientiously worked to lead Italy "to the highest destinies." The second article dealt with the theme of "The Book Crisis in France," a crisis that the young Assagioli saw also approaching Italy, and which he attributed to the lack of professionalism of publishers who were unable to stimulate the public with adequate reading materials.

THE UNIVERSITY YEARS

In November 1904 the Assagioli family moved to Florence. Roberto was to enroll in the university, and Florence is home of the Institute of Higher Studies, one of the most prestigious universities in Italy.[12] It had well-equipped laboratories for the study of anatomy, chemistry, physics, botanical gardens and astronomical observatories — everything needed to educate highly qualified scientists. The teaching staff was naturally at a high level.

Roberto chose to study medicine and surgery, and soon turned his attention to psychiatry. His interest in man's psyche, which was present even then, could not have been directed otherwise, since at that time psychology did not yet exist as a discipline in its own right. It was treated either in the faculties of liberal arts (especially philosophy) or in medicine (neurology and psychiatry). However, the Institute possessed a psychology laboratory attached to the Faculty of Letters and Philosophy and a Psychological Museum directed by the anthropologist Paolo Mantegazza (1831-1910). Assagioli was very interested in this and from 1906 to 1908 he held the position of librarian, which had previously been occupied by Giovanni Papini. At the time Italy was not at the forefront in the field of psychology, a discipline that was emerging in other European countries and in the United States.

Roberto Assagioli's early years in Florence were marked by very broad cultural interests and by his friendship with Giovanni Papini, who was seven years older and already well known in the literary field. At *Leonardo*, the magazine founded by Papini in 1903, Assagioli actively collaborated until its closing in 1907, and also contributed financial support for this publication, in whose editorial office young Florentine intellectuals met. The relationship with Papini, which was initially unequal (evidently Assagioli felt the greater maturity and education of

---

[12] *The Institute of Higher Studies had been founded in 1859 and later became part of the University of Florence, which was established in 1923.* —Ed.

his friend, which he respected),[13] over time became increasingly confidential and friendly. What united the two young people, in addition to the literary and cultural interests in general, was also curiosity about mediumistic sessions: we know they were planning sessions with the famous Neapolitan medium Eusapia Paladino,[14] in whom they both were very interested. Together they visited the *Biblioteca Occultista* [Occultist Library], which later became the *Biblioteca Filosofica* [*Philosophical Library*].[15]

Meanwhile Assagioli traveled to Rome and then Geneva, where he met psychologists Édouard Claparède[16] and Théodore Flournoy,[17] and he remained in contact with both for a long time. He would later publish some articles in the journal managed by Claparède.

Dating from this period is Assagioli's attention to Eastern philosophy, especially that of India, which to him appeared capable of overcoming that chasm between science and faith that divides our culture. Among the Indian works, Assagioli preferred the *Bhagavad-Gita*,[18] which he considered wonderful. He wrote that it demonstrated "how much the introspective psychology of the Indians, especially with regard to the higher states of consciousness, had reached such a point of complexity and depth that it far exceeded contemporary [Western] psychology." Assagioli saw deep psychological knowledge represented in yoga, and

---

[13] *i.e. Assagioli used the formal language address of* lei *with Papini.—Tr.*

[14] Eusapia Paladino (1854-1919) was a very famous medium. Apulian by birth, of modest origins, orphaned as a child, she went to work in Naples with a family and here her skills as a medium were revealed. In Naples she met Doctor Ercole Chiaia, who was passionate about spiritualism and who pointed her out to the major scholars of the time, including Cesare Lombroso, Charles Richet, Alexander Aksakov, who made Eusapia famous all over the world by doing sessions with her. The phenomena of the sessions were mainly physical: movement of furniture — even very heavy ones — levitations, moving of objects, complete lifting of the table, apparitions of ghost hands that left footprints on clay, cold winds, inexplicable lights. Enrico Morselli, Henri Bergson, Madame Curie, the journalist Luigi Barzini and many others also took part in her sessions: all remained convinced of the reality of the phenomena.

[15] *According to* A Snapshot of the Philosophical Library, *"A lively center of philosophical discussion, the Philosophical Library was started around 1903-1905 by those studying theosophy. Wanting to deepen their understanding of Oriental philosophy, library members loaned books, organized classes, conferences and published a bulletin." See* https://loveandwill.com/ *—Ed.*

[16] Édouard Claparède (1873-1940), was a Swiss doctor who specialized in psychology. He was influenced by William James; he founded and edited the *Archives de Psychology* with Théodore Flournoy.

[17] Théodore Flournoy (1854-1920), was a Swiss psychiatrist, also an admirer of William James, who was also in contact with C. G. Jung. He also studied mediums for a long time and published his studies on the medium Hélène Smith in a book entitled: *Des Indes à la planète Mars* (Paris 1900). Professor of psychology at the University of Geneva, he was known for his serious and rigorous methods.

[18] *The Bhagavad-Gita*, "The Song of the Blessed," is the greatest Indian religious poem. It dates back to the first centuries of our era.

the *Upanishads*[19] seemed to him to resolve the most sublime metaphysical and religious problems.

Roberto Assagioli was very precocious, and the distinctive and characteristic elements of his thought developed very early. His article "The New American Thought," which appeared in Issue No. 2 of 1907 of *Leonardo* (when Assagioli was just 19 years old . . .), already presents some of the fundamental aspects of the future thought of the founder of psychosynthesis: the will, seen as a tool to accomplish the transformation of oneself and consequently that of the external environment. Later we will discuss the will as the cornerstone of psychosynthesis; what is of interest now is to note how even then Assagioli saw in the will an energy capable of moving mountains — translated into psychological language, a force capable of modifying oneself and the surrounding world, if well-disciplined and directed.

His contact with the theosophical movement (apparently his mother was already interested in theosophy)[20] and in particular with the works of Annie Besant,[21] president of the International Theosophical Society, was certainly not unrelated to this orientation of his thinking. She had held a series of lectures in 1895 on the theme of "thought-forms,"[22] published in Italian under the title *Il tempio interno* [*The Interior Temple*].

In the "thought-forms" of theosophy, the concept of will can certainly be found as an element capable of shaping, if not actually creating, reality. "Nothing about man is as great as his mind," wrote Annie Besant in the essay whose English title was *The Control of Thought*. "The mind can be trained and will learn to choose what to think. This will prevent a thought from taking possession of you and becoming 'mistress in your home.'" Such thinking is essentially volitional.

---

[19] *The Upanishads*, or "Texts of Arcane Doctrine," are the earliest documents of Indian philosophical thought.

[20] *Theosophy* is a movement founded in 1875 by Helena Petrovna Blavatsky, a Russian occultist, who had received what she called "The Secret Doctrine," or the teaching that underlies all the great religions, from some Eastern initiates. In fact theosophy is very much influenced by the Hindu and Buddhist religions; it supports belief in reincarnation, karma and the wheel of existences until the final liberation. The theosophical movement advocates the union of all humanity in a universal brotherhood, and the need for perfection through the knowledge of the authentic laws of nature and man. Theosophy spread widely at the end of the last century and at the beginning of this one, and it still exists today all over the world.

[21] Annie Besant (1847-1933) was president of the Theosophical Society from 1907 until her death. A woman of great intellectual resources, she contributed greatly to the spread of theosophy and was the author of important works in this field.

[22] *Thought-forms*: this expression, ignored by mainstream psychology, refers to mental images that can be exteriorized and appear as real to the subject who projects them and also to other people. These are concepts found mainly in Eastern thought.

As we will see, Assagioli was active for a long time among theosophists, who were the first to rediscover the thought of the East for the Western world. One of the accomplishments of the founder of psychosynthesis is that he translated the philosophies and techniques of the East into scientific language suitable for modern people and acceptable to the academic world. He conveyed them through his psychosynthesis, which is essentially a guide to a process of inner growth, development and spiritual transformation.

For the young Assagioli, this was a time of much reading, which ranged across the most diverse fields: ancient and modern literature from all countries, which he could read in the original languages; Christian mysticism, with its rich harvest of moral and psychological teachings; occult themes and Eastern philosophies. In these wide-ranging interests, especially in esoterica and matters related to the East, Assagioli is very close to another great master of modern thought, C.G. Jung. Like Jung, Assagioli deeply felt the relationship between psychology and religion, and believed that there could be no true evolution of humanity if it was detached from spirituality and attention to transpersonal aspects.

However, before meeting C.G. Jung, Assagioli had already met Freud. In 1906 his article entitled "The Effects of Laughter and its Pedagogical Applications" appeared in issue No. 2 of the *Rivista di psicologia applicata alla Pedagogia e alla Psicopatologia* [*Journal of Psychology Applied to Pedagogy and Psychopathology*][23] edited by Cesare Ferrari of Bologna. The previous year, Assagioli had stayed in Vienna, had probably met Freud, or in any case had frequented the circles associated with him, and had read his essay "The Joke,"[24] deeply appreciated its value, and had taken inspiration for his own article from it. In it Assagioli writes that Freud had been the only one "who did not scorn the study of this subject" and to have sensed the psychological and educational effects of laughter: the future prophet of "smiling wisdom" could not but share this focus. The article, written at just 18 years of age, reveals Assagioli's nascent interest in the psychoanalytic movement and anticipates his life-long attitude: optimism, a sense of humor, joy.

In 1906 Assagioli often stayed in Rome, where he attended theosophical groups, and also went abroad several times, in particular to Geneva, where he met Flournoy

---

[23] *This journal, founded in 1905 in Bologna by Giulio Cesare Ferrari, was the first Italian scientific journal dedicated specifically to psychology. —Ed.*

[24] *"The Joke and Its Relation to the Unconscious" (in German 'Der Witz und seine Beziehung zum Unbewußten,") appeared in Italian as "Il Motto di Spirito" is an essay by Freud published in 1905. —Ed.*

and Claparède. He studied the psychology of William James[25] and deepened his knowledge of Freud's theories, which were increasingly affecting the Swiss psychological environment, naturally not without battles and internal conflicts. He had lengthy discussions with Théodore Flournoy about mediumship, a theme which aroused wide interest at the time. As we have seen, Flournoy had dealt with it in depth.

During this period Roberto Assagioli did not take many exams at the university; however he greatly expanded the horizon of his knowledge and personal culture. In addition to the activities already mentioned, he collaborated with Giuseppe Prezzolini, whom he had met in 1905 in connection with his work at *Leonardo*. Prezzolini urged him to contribute to a series on the mystics, initiated by Benedetto Croce:[26] *Poetae Philosophi et Philosophi Minores* [*Poets, Philosophers, and Minor Philosophers*]. Assagioli took charge of the translation, introduction and commentary for *Writings and Fragments of the Wizard of the North* by Georg Hamann, whom Goethe had called "the wizard of the north."[27] The text was published in 1908 by the publisher Perrella in Naples.[28] Hamann is a difficult writer, often using obscure language — a tormented, discontented and complex soul, who for Assagioli nevertheless presented aspects of "extraordinary psychological interest" and many ideas for a careful study of human nature. Thus, even while his literary interests occupied him so much in these years, Assagioli never abandoned his investigation of the human soul: psychological interests that would become increasingly focused and prominent.

But the collaboration with Prezzolini did not stop there. In 1908 they developed a plan to found a new magazine, which would be called *La Voce* [*The Voice*]. But collaboration was not without problems: Assagioli's contact with the theosophical circles did not excite Prezzolini. He wished to be completely autonomous and did not accept Assagioli's proposal, suggested by his father, to finance the magazine with a thousand lire in exchange for the position as secretary. He was probably afraid that Assagioli wanted to give the magazine a personal slant.

So *La Voce* was not financed by Assagioli, who nevertheless contributed a few articles, including the very important one on Freud which came out in February

---

[25] William James (1842-1910), American philosopher and psychologist, professor at Harvard University, considered one of the most significant exponents of American thought and the main theorist of pragmatism.

[26] *Benedetto Croce (1866-1952) was an Italian philosopher, historian, and politician.—Ed.*

[27] *Hamann (1730-1788) was one of the leading figures of post-Kantian philosophy. Goethe, Kierkegaard and others considered him to be the finest mind of his time. His work influenced later philosophers, including Herder and Hegel. —Ed.*

[28] *Assagioli's introduction to this publication, "Scritti e Framenti del Mago del Nord (Johann Geog Hamann)" is Doc. #23462 in the Assagioli Archives in Florence. —Ed.*

1910. This article already proposed the theme that would be treated by Assagioli at the conference on the sexual question organized by *La Voce* and held in Florence in November of that year. The essay, entitled "Transformation and Sublimation of Sexual Energies," met with the total disapproval from Prezzolini, who did not fail to express his opinion openly and very clearly. Prezzolini was never an admirer of psychoanalysis, with which Assagioli was much involved during those years.

Subsequently, relations between Prezzolini and Assagioli cooled further as Assagioli turned increasingly towards scientific activity. He did not abandon his previous literary interests and did not completely detach himself from the literary environment, from which he had drawn so much and which had certainly been formative for him. He pursued his medical studies with determination and, in preparation for his dissertation in psychiatry he attended the Burghölzli, the university psychiatric clinic in Zurich at the end of 1907. This opportunity had been offered to him by Claparède, who had stayed in Zurich to learn the technique of free association.[29]

He attended Burghölzli for two years, where C.G. Jung was also working and where Freudian theories had found acceptance (in that period Jung was considered Freud's heir-apparent by everyone; the separation occurred later, in 1913). At that time Assagioli made the decision to prepare his dissertation on psychoanalysis. In Italy there was little talk of psychoanalysis at the time: psychologists and psychiatrists worked on experimental, naturalistic and concrete premises and struggled to open up to new directions. In fact, Assagioli had to work hard to get his doctoral dissertation approved, because it followed the new direction created by Freud.

To better understand the situation, it is appropriate to briefly say something about the development of psychology, the psychoanalysis of Sigmund Freud and the positions of Jung and Assagioli.

Psychology arose by separating itself from philosophy and religion, of which it had always been a part. To better identify its own position, it eliminated the problems of the soul and transcendence from its field of investigation, and for a long time it used the experimental methods of medicine and physics. The object of these studies were memory, sensations, and psychosomatic reactions. This gave birth to behaviorism, which studied man from the point of view of psychopathology: more from the outside than from the inside. It had many strengths — and of course also certain limitations.

---

[29] Free association is a method that is based on the reaction time and on the content of the responses given to certain stimulus words, which leads to the discovery of emotional complexes, or autonomous contents of the unconscious, which act as disturbances. The method was developed by Freud, who used it after abandoning hypnosis.

Preceded by Pierre Janet,[30] who through his studies on "psychological automatism" had realized that many psychic activities are independent of a person's consciousness and that secondary personalities exist and act alongside the ordinary personality, Sigmund Freud (1856-1939) began an in-depth study of the unconscious processes; that is, the psychic activities of which the individual is not aware. For the study of the unconscious, Freud had previously used hypnosis, starting from the "cathartic method" of J. Breuer.[31] This consisted in bringing to the consciousness of the patient the forgotten facts that were the cause of the psychological disorder, making the patient relive them and thus relieving tension. Freud quickly realized that the same results could also be obtained with methods other than hypnosis, and developed the method of free association and dream analysis. He showed that many "repressions" due to resistances and defense mechanisms are the cause of mental disorders and morbid symptoms, and he claimed that many psychological and nervous disorders depend on the unconscious repression of sexual instincts.

Sigmund Freud's discoveries marked a real revolution: he distinguished the conscious, unconscious and preconscious, meeting much opposition, as one might logically expect, but also great acclaim by the most open and dynamic scholars.

Assagioli himself, in a lecture of March 1963,[32] listed the strengths and limitations of Freud's psychoanalysis: "The greatest merit of psychoanalysis was that of having contributed to the great discovery — or rediscovery — by modern psychology of the subconscious or psychic unconscious. It can be said that with this, psychology reached the third dimension. Previously it was "superficial," in that it dealt only with the psychological facts that arose on the surface of waking consciousness, ignoring what takes place in 'the depths.'"

For Assagioli, this great merit of psychoanalysis also constitutes its limitation:

> The major limitation of psychoanalysis is to have dealt only, or almost exclusively, with the lower aspects of the psyche. Yes, it is a 'depth psychology,' but always in a descending direction. Well, there is more than this aspect in our psyche; in the 'psychic building' there are not only the unhealthy subsoils to

---

[30] Pierre Janet (1859-1947) was a graduate in literature, philosophy and medicine, who taught at the Sorbonne and the College of France. He was one of the first to emphasize the dynamism and unity of psychic life, and dealt extensively with the unconscious, which he considered above all to be an automatic activity. A great scholar of hypnotic states, which was a logical extension of those studies, his work drew a variety of responses but also great acclaim from the most open and dynamic scholars.

[31] *Josef Breuer (1842-1925) was an Austrian physician who made discoveries in neurophysiology and whose work developed the "talking cure" or "cathartic method" which was the basis of his student Freud's psychoanalysis. —Ed.*

[32] *First Lesson in the Course of Lessons and Exercises in Psychosynthesis of 1963. —Ed.*

be restored, but also the various floors, and finally the luminous penthouses with large terraces, where the life-giving rays of the sun are taken in, and in the evening you can contemplate the stars. . . [33]

Freud himself admitted that he had always remained "in the basement of the building," and that he had not investigated the transcendent dimension, which he nevertheless sensed very clearly, as demonstrated by his own admission that he did not investigate it.

C. G. Jung was one of the first to welcome Freudian psychoanalysis but later distanced himself from it (in 1913), because he did not accept Freud's theory of sexuality and his concept of the unconscious. However, he made explorations in other dimensions: he discovered the collective unconscious and archetypes, the spiritual heritage of mankind, and gave great importance to the religious problem and the higher qualities of the psyche. Without Freud's groundwork, however, all this would not have been possible.

Jung called his psychological work "analytical psychology;" it is closer to psychosynthesis than [Freudian] psychoanalysis is, and the Jungian concept of "individuation" is not too dissimilar from the psychosynthetic vision of evolution of human consciousness, which must last a lifetime. More on that later.

Roberto Assagioli was thus one of the very first in Italy, if not the first, to seriously deal with psychoanalysis. And this was no small accomplishment, as initially psychoanalysis was strongly opposed there.

Professor Emilio Servadio,[34] one of the pioneers of psychoanalysis in Italy, recalls,

> The psychiatrists of the time did not understand psychoanalysis and did not welcome it. Standing opposed to it were also the idealist philosophy of [Benedetto] Croce and [Giovanni] Gentile, the leftists, fascists and the Catholic Church. The first years were very hard: we were very few in 1932, when Edoardo Weiss, a pupil of Freud, founded the Italian Psychoanalytic Society together with some collaborators, including Cesare Musatti and myself.[35]

---

[33] *Ibid.*

[34] *Emilio Servadio (1904-1994) was an Italian physician and psychoanalyst, one of the founders of the Italian Psychoanalytic Society.* —Ed.

[35] From a personal interview between Professor Servadio and the author.

By that time, however, Roberto Assagioli had already distanced himself from psychoanalysis for many years and had developed his personal psychological orientation.

But let's return to the formative years of the founder of psychosynthesis. In 1908, to complete his studies, Assagioli went to the clinic for nervous diseases in Munich and attended the courses of the psychiatrist Emil Kraepelin,[36] famous for his classification of early dementia. Kraepelin was anti-Freudian, but among the trainees (among whom there were several Italians), there was a lot of talk about Freud and Jung, even though not everyone shared their ideas. In Monaco Assagioli also got to know Ernest Jones, a follower of Freud and his future biographer,[37] and through him further deepened his knowledge of psychoanalysis.

This brings us to 1909, an important year for Roberto Assagioli, who for the first time expressed and systematized all the knowledge and discoveries he had acquired up to that time. In July he returned to the Burghölzli to prepare for his doctoral dissertation. In a letter of July 13 to Freud, C.G. Jung (with whom he had a close correspondence) wrote, "The migratory birds are returning; that is, the people who come to visit. Among these is an Italian acquaintance, a certain Dr. Assagioli of Florence, of the Florentine psychiatric clinic. Professor Tanzi[38] gave him psychoanalytic theory as his doctoral thesis. He is a very receptive young man who seems to have extensive medical knowledge and is in any case an enthusiastic follower, who penetrates the new territory with the momentum it takes. He wants to come and see you next spring . . ." Assagioli's presence in Zurich is thus confirmed, as well as his contact with Jung and the esteem he enjoyed thereafter: this enthusiastic young man is the "first Italian" to be seriously interested in psychoanalysis.

In August of the same year, Assagioli represented the Florentine Philosophical Circle at the International Congress of Psychology in Geneva, dealing in particular with the psychology of religious experiences and manifestations. Once again Assagioli expressed his interest in mysticism and related states of consciousness, as well as his openness to the cultural and philosophical traditions of the East. He

---

[36] *Emil Kraepelin (1856-1926) was a German psychiatrist, a founder of modern psychiatry and psychopharmacology who believed that the chief origin of psychiatric disease was biological or genetic malfunction.* —Ed.

[37] Ernest Jones (1879-1958), a Londoner, who taught in Toronto, Canada from 1908. He was co-founder of the American Psychoanalytic Society (1911) and the British Psychoanalytic Society (1913). He is the author of a fundamental biography of Freud: *Life and Work of Freud*, (in 3 volumes, 1953-1957).

[38] Eugenio Tanzi (1856-1934). A psychiatrist in Reggio Emilia and Florence. He was the author, together with Ernesto Lugaro, of a treatise on mental hygiene.

identified the basic differences between Eastern and Western mysticism, stating that Christians believe that these states of consciousness are experienced by divine grace, while Easterners think that a training undertaken voluntarily can allow one to reach one's own level. Apart from this difference, Assagioli says, the same experiences and manifestations are found in the mystics of all countries and religions. The states of consciousness of mysticism fall within the field of transpersonal psychology, which we will deal with later.

PSYCHAGOGY

Assagioli's dominant interest in this period is in education: he is just 21 years old, but the true essence of education is already clear in his mind. To talk about it, he retrieves a term used by Plato, *psychagogy*, meaning an education of the psyche, a learning process that does not stop at the child, the adolescent, or the teenager, but lasts a lifetime and fully embraces the whole personality. In this way Assagioli already clearly expressed the basic concepts of his *psychosynthesis* — a term which he used only much later. But the psychosynthetic process was very clear in his mind already in 1909, and he expressed it in his articles on "psychagogy."

Psychagogy is different from psychology in that, instead of focusing on the sick psyche, it turns turns its attention to the healthy psyche, to prevent the possibility of getting sick. This will be a basic characteristic of psychosynthesis: helping the healthy man to grow internally, to evolve throughout his life, giving ample space also to the spiritual, or transpersonal aspects, if we want to use this more neutral and scientific term.

In an article entitled "Toward a Modern Psychagogy,"published on February 25, 1909 in *La Voce*, the magazine edited by Giuseppe Prezzolini, the 21-year-old Assagioli expressed the now imperative need for a "radical reform of the current educational systems." He explained the reasons for the "negative outlook" given by [current] pedagogy:

> [The current educational system] does not consider the future man within the child, and stops his progress precisely at the age when it would begin to be truly fruitful — just when the young man is most capable of being educated, because on the one hand he has not yet lost the great flexibility of childhood, and on the other his more mature mind, his greater attention span, and his greater energy make him capable of profiting much more

than the child from help and advice — just then, modern education gives him nothing but a flood of information and imposes on him the obligation to be "obedient, composed, and diligent!"

"Psychagogy," Assagioli continues, "goes far beyond:"

It says that because man is never something defined, static, finished, but is in continuous formation, education must continue throughout life. The same psychological laws which regulate the psychic life of the child also regulate that of the adult and therefore the same methods that serve for the education of one serve, with appropriate adjustments, for the education of the other. The lower flexibility of the adult is amply compensated for by the greater strength and intelligence with which those methods can be applied by him and by his greater experience of life and self-knowledge, which make him avoid many mistakes into which the young man falls. . .

The concept of lifelong learning, the awareness of the need to cultivate and evolve oneself throughout one's life are therefore already present: Assagioli will return to it extensively later on; however, all of the seeds are already in the "psychagogy" of 1909.

Of great relevance from an educational point of view is a project presented in an article published in *La Voce* on June 3, 1909, entitled "Moral Education of University Students." It proposes a *Facultas Philosophica* accessible to students of all disciplines in which:

ethics and psychology are taught in a more humanistic and fruitful way than they currently are, in which courses on the history and philosophy of religions are established — courses that aim not only to provide interesting knowledge, but also to cultivate on the one hand the latent religiosity in many souls, and on the other the respect for every faith and the liberation from every narrow intolerance.

The student Roberto Assagioli worries about his classmates and writes

that the moral level among the students is very low, unfortunately does not need confirmation . . . But, note well, this certainly does not mean that young Italians are truly devoid of any nobility of feeling and behavior. It means instead that, gathered in universities, they lower themselves to the level of the worst, as happens in crowds, and do not feel elevated by the best, as happens among those who are an ideal community . . .

The situation is worrying, Assagioli continues, because "those who leave universities go on to become the so-called 'ruling classes,' and also because moral education is an indispensable requirement for a profession." Education is integral, not only to a profession but to life. This is a project that Assagioli pursued constantly, not through the creation of a special faculty [in the university] — that idea that was evidently still "utopian," even if very promising — but rather through his psychosynthesis.

In a letter written to Prezzolini the following year on November 10, 1910, Assagioli returned to the theme of education to clarify a misunderstanding deriving from an incorrect report that appeared in *La Voce*, regarding a speech he gave at a conference on the sexual question, which we will talk about below. The letter, in addition to clarifying the misunderstanding, presents the opportunity to express truly illuminating ideas on ethics and education:

> . . . I did not made any endorsement of the establishment of a chair of sexual psychology in the medical faculty. Such a proposal would be truly ridiculous, naive and impractical. Instead, I said that we should not believe that ordinary doctors, with all their naturalistic doctrine, are the most suitable people for sex education. But I said that students in medical schools should receive a psychological and moral training on the sexual issue . . . but I did not express myself at all on the precise way in which this could be done. Now I add that the simplest way would be that the professors of psychiatry or forensic medicine deal with it. If a new chair should be established, it should include the whole field of medical psychology, psychotherapy and professional ethics . . .

Thus, even from the medical perspective concerning the sexual problem, once again the young Assagioli faced the problem of ethics and the education of man with a surprising maturity for his age.

THE SEXUAL QUESTION

1909 was a very important year for the founder of psychosynthesis. In September he stayed in Zurich again to work on his dissertation on Freudian theories. Assagioli spoke of this in a letter to Giovanni Papini, dated August 27: "in a few days I will leave for Zürich, where I will stay in the mental hospital until the end of September to work on my interesting thesis on psychopathology (on Freud's theories etc.)." Since psychoanalysis was practically unknown in Italy at the time, Assagioli had struggled to obtain permission to do his dissertation on that topic with Professor E. Tanzi, with whom he completed his psychiatric internship at the San Salvi mental hospital in Florence.

In another letter to Papini, dated September 16 of the same year, this difficulty is expressed very clearly: "I can assure you that I have not chosen my present studies for reasons of expediency; on the contrary, they give me many difficulties and conflicts in the scientific field. I chose them because they seem to be the most suitable to satisfy my overwhelming need to know the mysteries of the human soul, and to use this knowledge for the liberation of souls." For Assagioli, the nascent science of psychology is *new* science, "the central science of the New Era, the science of man himself." It is evident that the young Assagioli had now found his way and decided to dedicate his life to psychology, the science that investigates the mysteries of the soul.

Soon, although not yet a graduate, Assagioli joined the Freudian Society of Zurich and was able to collaborate on reviews in the *Jahrbuch*: in a letter of January 19, 1910, Jung informed Freud of this directly. Thanks to his mastery of German, Assagioli also began an epistolary relationship with Freud, who expected him to spread the psychoanalytic movement in Italy.

The opportunity to do so was offered by *La Voce*, whose issue of February 10, 1910 was entirely dedicated to the sexual question: Assagioli contributed an article entitled "Sigmund Freud's Ideas on Sexuality," in which he presented to the Italian public three essays on Freud's theory of sexuality and took a position regarding the revolutionary discoveries of the Viennese master. The same concepts, expanded, were developed in the dissertation for his degree, which he obtained in July of the same year.

In this article Assagioli expressed his admiration towards Freud, whom he considered a brilliant creator of original methods for the study of the subconscious and sexual life. However, he then expressed certain reservations, inviting caution in the evaluation of Freud's ideas, while stressing their extraordinary practical importance. Assagioli also recognized Freud's courage to have dealt with an issue considered taboo at the time, highlighting real problems which can be understood and overcome only if well known.

Assagioli criticized the excessive emphasis Freud gave to sexuality, to the point of including psychic data that is generally distinct from it. He wrote that Freud gave importance to the instinctive and inferior side of sexuality and its aberrations without dealing with the "higher manifestations of love." Here Assagioli for the first time presented his concept of sublimation, as opposed to Freudian "repression." Sublimation is a "valuable faculty of the psyche," capable of "transforming blind instinctive forces into high emotional and spiritual energies." In this transformation, an important role belongs to the will, which can transform physical and emotional love into spiritual love. Furthermore, continued Assagioli, Freud excessively generalized child sexuality, exaggerating its scope and not distinguishing between normal children and neurotic children.

These reservations, expressed from the beginning, were those that later led to his separation from Freud, a process not too dissimilar from that which caused the much more sensational and significant break between Jung and Freud.

The article published in *La Voce* was of considerable importance. As David points out, Assagioli "was the first in Italy to introduce Freudian language and concepts in non-specialized cultural journals of wide scientific popularity, and with a decidedly positive attitude." [39]

A few months later, in November 1910, Assagioli participated in the first Italian Conference on the Sexual Question, organized by *La Voce* in Florence. Earlier we mentioned the letter of clarification written by Assagioli to Prezzolini. His presentation, "Transformation and Sublimation of Sexual Energies," was a development of the article published by *La Voce* and focused directly on the concept of sublimation. Assagioli spoke of the potential, inherent in everyone, of mastering one's passions by raising them to a higher level; in particular by transforming them into creativity. This process, which sometimes takes place on an unconscious level, must become conscious, and will result in a strengthening and expansion of our emotional and spiritual activities. The case of Dante, who sublimated his love for Beatrice in his writing of *The Divine Comedy*, and that of Wagner, who renounced his passion and used the corresponding psychic energy to write *Tristan and Isolde*, seemed to Assagioli the best examples of sublimation of an emotional love into spiritual love.

Freud had noted the possibility of transformation and sublimation. He wrote, "The very elements of the sexual instinct are characterized by their potential for

---

[39] Quoted from Ch. 19 of Eugenio Gaddini, *l movimento psicoanalitico in Italia* [*The Psychoanalytic Movement in Italy*]. Cortina Editore 1989.

THE FORMATIVE YEARS

sublimation, exchanging their sexual goal with a more distant, and socially more valuable goal. It is very likely that we owe the highest products of culture to the sum of the energies thus gained by our mental endeavors." [40] Freud, however, had stopped here, without going further.

Assagioli, after citing Dante, Wagner, and his contemporary Fogazzaro,[41] said,

> The same could be said of many philanthropists, educators and social workers. In these one can see a sublimation of maternal and paternal love, a true spiritual maternal or paternal instinct expressing itself in the care of bodies and souls (doctors, nurses, nuns, educators, social workers, spiritual guides). It is not necessary to think that one must be some sort of genius or a person of exceptional qualities to achieve such sublimation. Each of us can do this to some extent . . . The first requirement is the aspiration to achieve it, followed by a serious intent, a decision of the will, and an affirmation of what one is aspiring to. This acts as an effective spur, an order that psychological energies obey.[42]

After outlining the problem, Assagioli thus indicated the ways to deal with it:

> One must then move on resolutely to external action, throwing oneself into new activities likely to draw to one the energies for transformation, immersing oneself in those activities with a lively interest, with zeal and with enthusiastic commitment. It is then that all our energies flow in. The important thing is not to repress or try to suppress the lower energies in a separatist, hostile fashion, but to bring them under control with a calm firmness, at the same time giving free reign to expression of the higher energies. *It is not a question of loving less, but of loving better.* In modern times people often make the mistake of desensitizing themselves through intellectualism, sterile activism, ambition, and selfishness. They thus sever the links that exist between the various aspects of love.[43]
>
> One needs to love without fear: to love people, ideals, noble social causes — national and human — to love what is beautiful, what is best. The radiant,

---

[40] Quoted in Roberto Assagioli, *Transpersonal Development*, Astrolabe, Rome 1988, p. 178. *The English translation used here is from p. 201 of the English edition published by Inner Way Productions, 2007. —Ed.*

[41] *Antonio Fogazzaro (1842-1911) was an Italian novelist. —Ed.*

[42] Assagioli, *Transpersonal Development, op.cit.* p. 203, —Ed.

[43] Ibid.

ascendant power of this kind of love will attract to itself and absorb the sexual, passionate and emotional energies. Loving in this way, one must give and create. Give and create in different ways, depending on the circumstances and on one's own capacity, but always pouring out, giving oneself, radiating and expanding one's energies.[44]

The approach was clear and precise, with a determination and clarity of purpose that are amazing in a young man just 22 years old.

THE MEDICAL DEGREE

Before the conference in Florence, at the end of March 1910, Assagioli had attended the Nuremberg congress in which the greatest exponents of the psychoanalytic movement took part, including Freud and Jung, who had just returned from their trip to America,[45] and Adler. In the report he wrote on the conference for the *Journal of Applied Psychology*, Assagioli stated that Freud's presentation on "the future possibilities of psychotherapy" had, logically, been the most awaited and important.

On the occasion of the congress, the International Psychoanalytic Association was founded, based in Zurich. It was chaired by C.G. Jung until 1913, the year of his break with Freud. Assagioli, the only Italian among 19 Swiss, became a member. As we have already mentioned, Assagioli was the first to introduce psychoanalysis in Italy and to work for its diffusion, albeit with some caution and reservations.

On July 1, 1910 Assagioli presented his doctoral dissertation, entitled "Psychoanalysis," and discussed it with Professor Tanzi, thus concluding his university studies. After graduation, he intended to devote himself to psychotherapy, of which, as he wrote in a letter of August 6 to Giovanni Papini from Gressoney (where he was on vacation), "It promises great benefit for patients and valuable observations and experiments for myself."

1910 and 1911 are the years of Assagioli's most intense participation in the psychoanalytic movement, with contributions to the journals founded by Freud,

---

[44] *Ibid. pp. 203-204.*

[45] Freud and Jung's trip to America was organized by Ernest Jones, then director of the psychiatric clinic of the University of Toronto, in order to make psychoanalysis in the United States known through conferences in a medical environment. During the trip, which was very successful, both Freud and Jung were awarded honorary degrees from Clark University in Worcester, Massachusetts.

Zentralblatt für Psychoanalyse[46] and *Jahrbuch far psychoanalytische und psycbopathologische Forschung.*[47] In *Jahrbuch* no. 1/2 of 1911, in an article entitled "Freud's teachings in Italy," Assagioli also expresses the reasons for the lack of interest in psychoanalysis in Italy:

> Strangely, Freud's teachings have not aroused great interest in Italy, although in my judgment the Italian spirit, thanks to its liveliness and finesse, should be accessible to the subtle thought operating in psychoanalysis. The causes of this neglect are however understandable if one considers the current status of psychiatric research in Italy. Overall, it can be said that Italian researchers in this field are divided into two groups. The first follows a direction that can be defined as clinical and deals with the symptomatology and classification of psychoses. The other, by contrast, follows the anatomical directive and mainly deals with histological and biochemical problems. Thus it happens that authentic psychopathological research suffers considerable neglect, apart from some special fields, such as mediumship and psychic abnormalities in children: this latter aspect because of its particular practical interest . . .

RELATIONS WITH C.G. JUNG

After graduation, Assagioli spent a new period in Zurich at the Burghölzli clinic to study with Eugen Bleuler, discoverer of schizophrenia. In the previous year Jung had left the clinic, where he had been chief physician, due to misunderstandings with Bleuler and also due to overwork. After his marriage in 1903, Jung had lived for a few years at the clinic in an apartment reserved for the chief physician, then he had built a house in Küsnacht, near Zurich, and moved there. Here he started working with private clients, and it was here that Assagioli visited him.

Many years after his meetings with Jung, Assagioli recalled, "Jung affably welcomed visitors who came from all over, and I keep alive the memory of the animated conversations I had with him in his large study, with walls all covered with books and full of curious exotic objects."

The relationship with Jung was always extremely cordial, and the friendship was cemented by the common interest in psychoanalysis, as well as in paranormal

---

[46] *Central Journal for Psychoanalysis.*

[47] *Yearbook for Psychoanalytic and Psychopathological Research.*

phenomena, astrology, and Eastern philosophies. Jung had written his dissertation in 1902 on "Psychology and Pathology of So-called Occult Phenomena," using material from séances in which he had participated as a young man, in which his cousin acted as a medium. He himself possessed qualities of sensitivity, and in his long life he had the opportunity to experience many paranormal phenomena firsthand.

With reference to the Jung-Assagioli relationship, it is curious that the term "psychosynthesis," which Assagioli did not use at the time, at least officially (he spoke at that time, as we have seen, of "psychagogy"), was in a certain sense proposed by Jung. In a letter to Freud, which bears two dates, April 2 and April 12, 1909, we find this very significant phrase: *If psychoanalysis exists, there must also be a "psychosynthesis" that builds a future according to the same laws* — a clear reference to the evolution of the psyche, to a forward-looking and more final vision, which later found its own place in what Jung called his "analytical psychology," and even more clearly and widely, in Assagioli's psychosynthesis.

The good relations between Jung and Assagioli lasted a long time. In 1946, after the end of the world war, Assagioli wrote a letter to Jung to ask him to provide help concerning his son Ilario, who was ill with tuberculosis. The letter denotes the lively sympathy and mutual respect between the two colleagues:

January 1946
Distinguished and dear colleague,

Mindful of the gracious welcome you provided when I passed through Zurich in 1939 returning (imprudently!) from England to Italy, I take the liberty of writing to you to give you my news and to ask you for a small favor.

My family and I have come out alive from the whirlwind of war, but we have suffered persecutions and dangers, as I mentioned in the "Letter to Friends" which I enclose.[48] In it, however, I do not speak of a serious difficulty and complication that we had during the war years, and the serious illness of my son, who is suffering from pulmonary tuberculosis. However, he has endured the hardships surprisingly well and has improved much since 1944.

Now a very favorable opportunity has presented itself for him to hasten his recovery: *La Fédération Européenne de Secours aux Etudiants* [the European Student Relief Federation] will almost certainly include him in the group of

---

[48] We will reproduce this "letter to friends" in the second part of this book, The one dedicated to the years of maturity.

twenty Italian students to whom it offers hospitality and care for six months in the University Sanatorium of Leysin. He very much wants me to accompany him there and I would also like to do it to talk to colleagues at the Sanatorium about the treatment, etc. It seemed difficult for me to obtain permission to enter from the Swiss authorities, but the Committee of the *Fédération* hopes to obtain it by appointing me, as a doctor, to accompany the whole group of students. But perhaps the federal authorities will ask for information and references on my behalf from some well-known Swiss citizen. So I allowed myself to give your name and if you are asked about me I hope you will report that I am not an "undesirable" guest for a short stay in Switzerland!

Apart from all this — given that, as you know, I have always followed your work as a brilliant pioneer in the field of psychology with great appreciation and admiration — I would like to know what your activities have been during these years and if you have published new writings, so that I can get them during my trip to Switzerland.

Please excuse the inconvenience and accept my warmest wishes and cordial greetings.

Your devoted
Roberto Assagioli

Years later, in 1966, Assagioli gave three lectures at the Institute of Psychosynthesis in Florence which presented the similarities and differences between Jung's concepts and methods and those of psychosynthesis. "Jung," wrote Assagioli, "among all psychotherapists is the one who is closest to the position and practice of psychosynthesis."

He had been, Assagioli continued,

a brilliant investigator and therapist of the human soul, who most courageously did [this work] with a mind free from preconceptions and academic constraints . . . He had a profound human sensibility, an intense thirst for knowledge, an admirable honesty and intellectual modesty, a sincere recognition of his own shortcomings . . . and also those of others . . .

It would take too long to quote everything that Assagioli wrote in his three lectures: [he discusses] many analogues; for example the "vivid sense of the complexity of the human psyche" and the "relative autonomy of the various psychic contents and the existence of different 'subpersonalities.'" But [he also mentions] differences: Jung, for example, never mentions the will, a determining element of Assagioli's psychosynthesis, and does not pay sufficient attention to social aspects, to interpersonal and group relationships.

Like Assagioli, Jung had the great virtue ("perhaps his greatest virtue") of having "recognized and proclaimed (almost alone among modern psychologists) the reality and importance of spiritual needs." Indeed, Jung had observed that many neuropsychic disorders depend on the "lack of fulfillment of this need, on its repression."

Jung's description of the "individuation" process — that is, the path that leads to one's Self, to self-realization — was also highly appreciated by Assagioli. For Jung, the individuation process constitutes the authentic meaning of human life, the engine of evolution, and as such it can never be totally achieved. In fact, he wrote, "Personality as a full realization of the totality of our being is an unattainable goal. It is an ideal, and therefore a guide." Jung believed that alchemical writings, many myths and legends, especially the great, adventurous journeys of heroes (the Odyssey, for example), were actually descriptions of the personal individuation process. As we shall see, Assagioli's psychosynthesis also moves in this direction and supports the harmonious development of the personality and of all psychic qualities.

PSICHE

In April 1911, during the philosophy congress held in Bologna, Assagioli had the opportunity to present the psychoanalytic doctrines again, this time examining the concept of the subconscious, which seemed to him to be the most significant element of the Freudian theories. Even later, writing on psychoanalysis, Assagioli always recognized this great achievement of Freud:

> Psychoanalytic investigations have shown that the choices and actions we carry out, from the most futile to the most serious and decisive, are often due to reasons or determined by influences we are not aware of. That is, while we believe we are acting on the basis of conscious and rational motives, we are instead driven by impulses deriving from impressions, experiences, emotions, suggestions (not infrequently dating back to childhood) that we did

not realize we were undergoing or that we have forgotten, but who remain alive and active in our unconscious . . . [49]

In subsequent years Assagioli increasingly focused his interest on psychology, gradually lessening his direct involvement with literature, although he retained literary and musical interests throughout his life. Among other things, Assagioli maintained friendships with writers and artists from all over the world. Now, however, he concentrated all his energies on an ambitious project: the creation of a magazine dedicated to psychology. He himself made the announcement to Prezzolini in a letter dated April 26, 1911. Prezzolini asked for financial help for a literary project, and Assagioli had to reply that unfortunately he could not support him, as his father, who was usually very generous with initiatives of this kind, had declined the invitation to collaborate. Assagioli writes in his letter:

> He is now planning to provide the means for carrying out a fairly vast scientific program of mine, of which (I tell you in confidence) a periodical publication is part . . . I feel increasingly called to carry out my activity in the scientific field. I believe I am doing useful work for Italian culture by trying to encourage psychological and psychopathological studies and the application of psychotherapeutic methods among us — studies and applications in which the comparison with what has been successfully done abroad is particularly humiliating for us . . .

---

[49] From the lecture of 1963 cited earlier.

1. Roberto Assagioli in his studio, in his last years

2. Roberto Assagioli about 1910.

3. Assagioli in New York, 1937.

4. One of the little cards with the "evocative words".

5. A photo of Assagioli in his maturity.

6. Assagioli on his way to the U.S.A.

7. On the same occasion, Assagioli with his niece,
Donatella Ciapetti.

8. Roberto Assagioli (left) with Papini and Vailati,
in the Leonardo editorial office (c. 1908-1909).

9. Roberto Assagioli surrounded by his students.

10. The villa at Via San Domenico, 16 in Florence, where the Institute of Psychosynthesis is located.

11. Roberto Assagioli's studio with his desk.

Psiche, a "magazine of psychological studies," was founded in early 1912 and was published in Florence quarterly until 1915. The magazine's program [range of interest] was very broad and can be read on the fourth cover page of the magazine itself:

1) Psychology and philosophy, 2) Physiological and experimental psychology, 3) Comparative psychology and psycho-biology, 4) Pathological psychology, 5) Child and pedagogical psychology, 6) Character psychology (ethology) and psychagogy, 7) Collective and social psychology, 8) Ethnic psychology, 9) Supernormal psychology, 10) Psychoanalysis and study of the subconscious, 11) Psychology of religion, 12) Aesthetic psychology, 13) Sexual psychology, 14) Forensic psychology, 15) Study of autobiographies and contributions to psychology found in poetic and literary works, 16) History of Western psychology, and 17) Eastern psychology.

A vast program, which could not be completed because the magazine did not have a long life. However, leafing through the vintage issues of *Psiche*, one realizes the multiplicity of the topics covered. The directors were professors Enrico Morselli from Genoa, Sante de Sanctis from Rome and Guido Villa from Pavia. Assagioli himself was editor in chief. *Psiche* can be considered the first example of topics in psychology being published for a large audience, rather than only for specialists.

Assagioli contributed to the magazine both with his work as editor-in-chief and with articles. I mention a few: one on Psychology and Psychotherapy; one on Alfred Adler and one very curious piece on the famous "thinking horses of Elberfeld," a phenomenon that at the time caused a lot of sensation and involved characters of considerable importance, including Father Agostino Gemelli.[50]

In his article "Psychology and Psychotherapy" published in Issue no. 3 of 1913, Assagioli affirmed the importance of these disciplines for man and reconstructed their history and development. He stressed the great flowering of modern work: the writings of scholars such as Breuer, Freud, Jung, Adler, Dubois, Prince have produced an extensive bibliography. With obvious discomfort Assagioli observed that:

---

[50] *Agostino Gemelli, (1878–1959) was an Italian Franciscan friar, physician and psychologist, who was also the founder and first Rector of Università Cattolica del Sacro Cuore [Catholic University of the Sacred Heart] of Milan.—Ed.*

Italy has unfortunately not made any significant contribution to this movement. On the contrary, given the great scarcity and little importance of the publications in this area, it can be said that only a faint and distant echo of it has come to us, to which the doctors, who are busy with other matters, have given little attention — with rare exceptions.

After stressing the importance of psychotherapy, Assagioli concludes,

I take the liberty of encouraging doctors, especially the young ones, to deal with psychotherapy much more than they have done so far, especially in Italy. I assure them that if they study it seriously and practice it ardently, it will give them great scientific and professional as well as human satisfactions. Thus it will be possible to obtain an ever deeper understanding of psychic life, and at the same time an ever greater effectiveness in the fight against very serious and painful evils — indeed, in a certain aspect, the most terrible ones, because they undermine what is most valuable in man: his soul.

The second article outlines the personality of Alfred Adler, physician and psychologist, who was at first a follower of Freud. Later Adler followed his own path and created his own Individual Psychology, the aim of which is the study of the "life plan" of each individual. While Freud argues that our psychic activity generally has its origin in libido (sexual instinct understood in a broad sense), Adler identifies the "will to power," the desire for supremacy, as the motive for human actions. While acknowledging the merits of both Freud and Adler, Assagioli maintains in an article in *Psiche* (no. 4, July-September 1914) that those two thinkers "do not sufficiently recognize the importance and dignity of altruistic ends and superior aesthetic feelings, both moral and religious. As pessimistic as we can be about human nature," he continues, " the history of humanity shows in an incontrovertible way that selfless love, compassion, self-denial, and the spirit of sacrifice all *exist*, and that higher, ultra-personal values have often induced men to perform extraordinary acts and to deny the satisfaction of their selfish desires for pleasure and power." In these words there is already much of Assagioli's psychosynthesis.

The article on thinking horses is the most unusual; it is also very interesting in that it signifies the openness of the magazine to unusual issues and reveals Assagioli's interest in everything that has to do with "mystery," understood in the highest and noblest sense of the term. To discuss this article it is first necessary to say something about the horses themselves.

In the German town of Elberfeld in 1890, school teacher Wilhelm von Osten had tried to give an elementary education to his stallion Hans, which showed remarkable intelligence. Hans had learned to obey certain words, to count pins, to beat with his hoof the one-digit numbers that his master wrote on a blackboard. When Hans died, von Osten tried another horse, Hans the Second, who managed to perform small mathematical operations with one- or two-digit numbers and to count objects. In 1905 Karl Krall, an Elberfeld jeweler, picked up the legacy of his old friend von Osten and continued the experiments on a larger scale with six horses, four Arabian stallions, a pony and a blind horse named Berto.

Then a new and disconcerting phenomenon occurred: while the two Hans had managed to calculate within the limits of a child's intelligence, the new horses proved capable of making calculations higher than what an adult person can memorize: from high-digit numbers that Krall wrote on the board they extracted up to the fifth root.[51] The phenomenon, made known by Krall himself in a publication, aroused much interest and several men of science went to Elberfeld remaining convinced of the authenticity of the facts: among them Professor Claparède of the University of Geneva, the Belgian writer Maurice Maeterlinck, Professor Beredka of the Pasteur Institute of Paris, Father Gemelli and others. Assagioli went there in 1912, together with William Mackenzie, a biologist, philosopher and scholar of parapsychology, and obtained from the most gifted stallion, Muhammed, immediate solutions to some operations he suggested, for example $\sqrt[4]{28,561}= 13$, and $\sqrt[3]{91,125} = 45$.

In the article published in *Psiche* (no. 6, 1913) Assagioli described the facts and tried to give an explanation to the phenomenon by putting forth various hypotheses (subconscious activity of horses, automatic brain, telepathy, intelligence). Replying to critics that they denied everything to the bitter end without ever having been to Elberfeld and without having even read what had been published on the matter, he concluded:

We observe animals with patience and educate them with love; science will in no way lose its seriousness and rigor; it will lose only the presumption with which only man has been called 'sapiens.' And humbly stooping to interrogate the lower beings, he may perhaps better understand the obscure

---

[51] *In mathematics, a root is a number which when multiplied by itself a number of times gives a certain result. For example the square root of 4 is 2 (2 x 2 =4) and the fourth root of 16 is 2 (2 x 2 x 2 x 2 =16 or $\sqrt[4]{16}= 2$). —Ed.*

message of the human spirit; he can more easily illuminate another small shadow of the great veil of mystery.[52]

These words demonstrate all of Assagioli with his rigor, his humility, and his openness towards all that is.

During the years he worked on *Psiche*, Assagioli further developed his concepts, defined his psychosynthesis, and broke away from Freud. Despite having distanced himself from Freud, Assagioli always had a great respect for him. On May 14, 1974, a few months before his death, he received a letter from Prezzolini in which the writer asked for consent to include one of the old articles Assagioli had written on Freud for *La Voce* in an anthology. Assagioli agreed immediately, but invited him to add this note: "Dr. Assagioli has asked us to tell those who do not know him that since [this article was written], his ideas on psychoanalysis have changed a great deal. It was a starting point or a 'springboard' for him to develop the concepts and practice of psychosynthesis."

Assagioli always maintained that the concepts of psychoanalysis are initially indispensable as techniques for exploring the unconscious. Studying the [Assagioli] Archive in Florence, I happened to find one of those handwritten notes on which Assagioli wrote down thoughts, ideas, sensations, intuitions. It read, "A professor of psychiatry in a major Italian city has Freud's books, but she said, 'I haven't had time to read them yet!!' (in 1949 !!)" For Roberto Assagioli it was evidently inconceivable that anyone involved in psychiatry and psychotherapy did not know Freud and did not take his discoveries and his theories into account .[53]

It is important to mention here, in connection with the journal *Psiche*, the founding of the "Circle of Psychological Studies" in Florence in 1913 by Assagioli and the scholars who revolved around *Psiche*. The association's aim is very broad. In fact, we read in its Charter:

Art. 1 - An association is established in Florence among those interested in psychology, with the name of "Circle of Psychological Studies."

Art. 2 - The Circle aims to cultivate and promote psychological studies, understood in the widest sense, both in their principles and especially in their

---

[52] *Assagioli's two articles (1912 and 1913) on the thinking horses are found as Doc.#23125 and 23193 in the Assagioli Archives. They have been translated into English in draft typed manuscripts found in the papers of Psychosynthesis Research Foundation. The quotation is an edited version of the latter.* —Ed.

[53] *This editor has discovered numerous essays and lectures by Assagioli given over the course of his life in which he made a careful distinction between the practice of psychoanalysis, which he thought was indispensable, and the specific theories (especially the sexual theories) propounded by Freud, some of which he rejected.* —Ed.

applications to the most diverse disciplines. The Circle will make special efforts to bring various students together, to coordinate their activity and to promote collective work (experiments; investigations; bibliographic collections; discussion of terminology, etc.).

A very vast program, as can be seen, which was abruptly interrupted by the outbreak of the First World War, which also marked the end of *Psiche*.

CHAPTER 2
THE YEARS OF MATURITY

> Life is a real school of 'initiation.'
> Every fact, every external or internal event
> is an exercise, a task, a test (trial), or exam.
> — R. Assagioli: *Educating the Man of Tomorrow*

WORLD WAR I. MARRIAGE AND MOVE TO ROME

The outbreak of the First World War interrupted a great flurry of initiatives. The magazine *Psiche*, to which Roberto Assagioli had dedicated so much work and love, had to be suspended, and the "Circle of Psychological Studies" also closed its doors. Like many of his colleagues, Roberto Assagioli was also conscripted into the military, and served as a medical lieutenant.

Little is known about [Assagioli during] these years, or of those immediatcly after the war. Psychotherapist Piero Ferrucci, who was very close to the father of psychosynthesis in the last years of his life, says that Assagioli never spoke of that period. He said only that he had never fired a weapon — indeed, he had never even carried a revolver. He had made one of soap and painted it black and in this way he gave the impression of being armed. On the eve of the Second World War, Assagioli was accused of "pacifist activities" — not without cause — and for this unusual reason he had to serve a month in prison.

After the war, everything slowly started again. As mentioned, very little is known of the years immediately following the war. Assagioli left no note in this regard and there is no longer anyone alive who knew him closely in those years and could relate anything. Certainly he resumed his activity and his studies and began to pursue the profession of psychotherapist.

According to Ms. Luisa Maccaferri Lunelli, a frequent visitor to the Assagioli family from 1933 onwards and who was a close friend of both Roberto and his wife and son, I learned that Assagioli had a first marriage which was brief and childless, ending in divorce. Of this first marriage Assagioli said in his unfinished autobiography that his first wife was a patient who had been referred to him, coming from a very simple family with problems of personality dissociation. Assagioli tried to be "her Pygmalion," but to no avail: their characters and life plans were too different. The separation was not technically difficult because they had only a civil marriage, although it was painful for both of them and presented quite a few complications. Assagioli adds that the separation was "the right thing for both of us, because she found an army officer who married her and they had three children and led a normal life with him, so that settled her."[54] The marriage, Assagioli continues, had taken place immediately after World War I.

His second marriage took place in 1922. Nella Ciapetti, the bride, was Catholic, but also a follower of theosophy as Roberto's mother had been. She owned a villa with surrounding land in Capolona, in the Arezzo countryside, where the family spent the summer holidays for decades. Nella was a woman of confidence and solid temperament who personally managed the family business. From the marriage with Nella, which lasted over 50 years,[55] Roberto Assagioli's son Ilario was born in 1923.

In 1926 we find the Assagioli family in Rome. The reasons for the move from Florence to the capital are not known, but they can perhaps be identified in the different situation of Rome compared to Florence. The less provincial, more open, freer Roman environment could offer better social and cultural possibilities, more interesting encounters, more space to carry out one's work and ideas. It should also not be forgotten that Assagioli cultivated esoteric interests, and in Rome it would have also been easier for him to pursue them. In any case, Roberto Assagioli moved to Rome with his wife and son and settled in a building in Via Antonio Bosio, a side street of the Nomentana, which at the time was almost rural.

THE BIRTH OF PSYCHOSYNTHESIS

The years between the two wars were those in which Roberto Assagioli's thought was deepened and integrated. These were years of intense work, study, reading; of international meetings and friendships, travels, and experiences in very different fields: years in which Assagioli's ideas, which had already been precociously outlined since early youth, were defined and took on their characteristic configuration.

Psychosynthesis was born from psychagogy. It is a psychotherapeutic method that aims at the overall training and restructuring of mankind that has broad

---

[54] *Quoted from the English language edition of* Roberto Assagioli In His Own Words, *p. 46.* —Ed.

[55] *This is a correction to the original text, which read "forty years."* —Ed.

applications in family and school education, interpersonal relationships, and in the enrichment and empowerment of personality as well as in psychotherapy. Assagioli developed psychosynthesis after having experimented with various psychotherapeutic methods. Into it he poured all his deep insights and his great openness towards all the human sciences and spiritual disciplines.

Roberto Assagioli did not write much, in the sense that the books he left are very few and were written only in old age. Two of these were originally written in English, a language he knew as well as Italian. They are *Psychosynthesis. A Manual of Principles and Techniques*, released in the United States in 1965;[56] and *The Act of Will*, released in New York in 1973, a year before the author's death. There is also *Psicosintesi: Per l'armonia della vita* (*Psychosynthesis: For the Harmony of Life*), a collection of essays from 1932 revolving around the theme of self-knowledge and permanent education, published in 1971 by the Mediterranean Editions of Rome.[57] And finally *Lo sviluppo transpersonale*, published in 1988 by Astrolabio, a collection of Assagioli's "spiritual" writings edited by Maria Luisa Girelli Macchia.[58]

Roberto Assagioli wrote mainly lectures and short essays, most of which have not been published, but copies can be requested from the Institute of Psychosynthesis, Via San Domenico, 16, in Florence.[59] There are [over] three hundred titles on the most diverse subjects and also handwritten notes in many different languages, arranged in order in the Archives by the Assagioli study commissioned by Piero Ferrucci, of whom I spoke at the beginning: there is a goldmine of wisdom, knowledge, goodness, and humor, which waits to be discovered.[60] Assagioli's writings therefore do not yet constitute a well-defined and finished collection of works, but are a sort of "Saint Patrick's Well" (to use an unscientific but effective expression) from which will be possible to draw for a long time.[61]

As early as 1926, however, Assagioli had published a booklet in English entitled *Psychosynthesis. A New Method of Healing*, in which he presented the principles of the

---

[56] The Italian edition, edited by the Astrolabio in Rome, was published in 1973 as *Principi e metodi della psico sintesi terapeutica*.

[57] This book was translated into English by Catherine Ann Lombard and published in 2022 as *Creating Harmony in Life: A Psychosynthesis Approach*, published by the Istituto di Psicosintesi in Florence. —*Ed*.

[58] *This book was translated into English in 1991, and was retranslated into English as* Transpersonal Development: The Dimension Beyond Psychosynthesis *and published by Inner Way Productions in Scotland in 2007*. —*Ed*.

[59] *As of this writing, this editor/translator and others have translated many of these lectures and essays into English, which are being made available online*. —*Ed*.

[60] *The Archives have been organized by a group of dedicated volunteers, who have enhanced the accessibility of the documents by digitizing most of the Archive. It is available online at* https://www.archivioassagioli.org/index.php. —*Ed*.

[61] *"Saint Patrick's Well" (actually in Orvieto in Italy) suggests an endless cave*. —*Ed*.

complex body-mind relationships that are the basis of psychosomatic medicine, of which Assagioli was one of the pioneers. In that same year Roberto Assagioli founded the Institute of Culture and Psychic Therapy in Rome, which in 1933 became the Institute of Psychosynthesis.

We will devote another section of this book to the issues that were important to Assagioli; however, for now it is appropriate to anticipate some basic principles of psychosynthesis. Assagioli was a forerunner in many fields: he was, as we have seen, the first representative in Italy of Freudian psychoanalysis, from which he then broke away to pursue his own way, and he was one of the founders of psychosomatic medicine. Already in the 1920s he spoke of music therapy and color therapy. He was an originator of humanistic-existential psychology, in the sense that from the first decades of the century he spoke of a psychology of health; that is, he saw man not only as a bearer of conflict and complexes, but also of healthy potential and needs for normality. Finally, he was a precursor of transpersonal psychology, which developed in the 1970s and which considers states of consciousness that go beyond the ego and that concern "spiritual" or "transpersonal" experiences.

To give an initial idea of Assagioli's thought and his concept of the human psyche, it is appropriate to resort to a very significant image. Assagioli said, "A picture is worth a thousand words," and to represent the psyche as he conceived it he designed an egg, a perfect cosmic egg, at the center of which he placed the "I", or conscious self. The egg is then divided into three sections: at the bottom there is the "cellar," or the lower unconscious center of psychic activities that preside over organic life and coordination, physiological functions, primitive instincts, psychic complexes, dreams and imaginative activities of an elementary type. At the center is the middle unconscious, where the processes of experience take place, future activities are prepared, and where the large archive of memory is located. At the top there is the "attic," the upper floor, the transpersonal unconscious; that is, all those superconscious contents of which we are not aware, the area from which the intuitions, the higher artistic, philosophical and scientific inspirations, the altruistic impulses, the states of illumination, contemplation, and ecstasy come; this is also the source of supernormal and paranormal powers.

At the apex of the superconscious there is a "star," representing what modern psychology calls the Self, and which corresponds to the traditional concept of soul: our deepest and most authentic identity, understood not as an ideal destination, but as an experiential reality of which the "I" is a reflection. The entire egg is immersed in the collective unconscious, the infinite reservoir of group or mass energy, with which there is a relationship of mutual interaction.

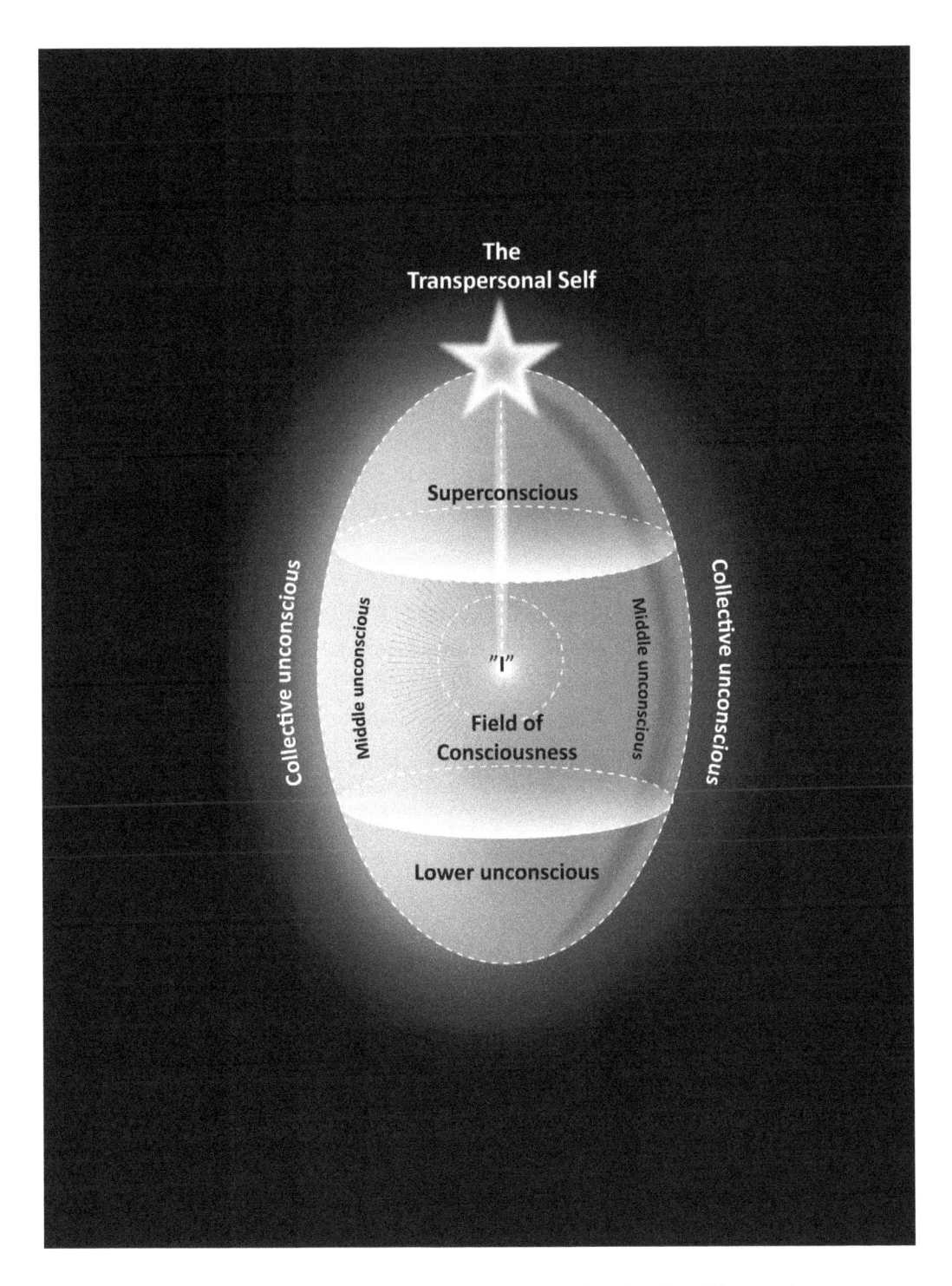

Assagioli's Concept of the Human Psyche: the 'Egg Diagram'

Assagioli's vision was certainly wider than that of Freud, from whom he took his initial inspiration, and was quite close to that of C. G. Jung, with whom — as we have seen — Assagioli had cordial relations, cemented also by their common interest in esotericism, Eastern culture, and religion.

RELIGION, ESOTERICISM AND EASTERN SPIRITUALITY

Roberto Assagioli was always eager to keep his esoteric and spiritual interests separate from his scientific interests; however, it is undeniable that elements derived from theosophy, esotericism, and Eastern disciplines converge in his psychosynthesis. Assagioli's achievement is to have been able to translate these contributions into a form and language accessible to us Westerners and conforming to our mentality.

Coming from a Jewish family, Roberto Assagioli always belonged formally to this religion, for which he had the utmost respect. He had a relationship of great esteem and friendship with Jewish philosopher, humanist and anthropologist Martin Buber, who throughout his life sought understanding between East and West, between Jews and Arabs. A great prophet of modern Judaism, Martin Buber sought to renew the Jewish message beyond hatred and all the problems associated with Zionism, as well as to promote dialogue between Christians and Jews, and international understanding. Assagioli felt in deep harmony with him.

In all probability, Assagioli shared the Jewish Messianic expectation. In one of his writings entitled, "The Universal Messianic Expectancy,"[62] we read, "In Judaism, the Messianic expectation has a central place. As a foremost exponent of Jewish thought and spirituality, Martin Buber, said, 'The messianic expectation is the most profound idea of Judaism.'" However, he compared the Jewish Messianic expectation to the return of Christ expected by Christians, which held that this return would be preceded "by a period of wars and desolations, called 'apocalyptic,' because of the vivid description contained in the [New Testament Book] *Apocalypse*."[63]

His connection to Judaism and the great respect he always had for Christianity did not diminish his interest in Eastern philosophy and spirituality. We have seen that his mother and his wife were theosophists, and Assagioli also participated in

---

[62] Published under the pseudonym of "Considerator" in the magazine *Verso la luce* and reprinted in the text *Le vie dello spirito* (Milan 1992) which contains his collected his writings from the years 1963-1974.

[63] *This essay was also published under his own name in English as* The Universal Messianic Expectancy *in* The Beacon *in 1952, from which the quotations from this essay are taken.* —Ed.

this movement of thought. Some things should be said about theosophy. The term derives from the Greek (*theòs* = God and *sofia* = wisdom) and therefore means divine wisdom. Its origin is very ancient, as the word was coined in the third century A.D. by Ammonius Saccas (175-243), Plotinus' teacher and founder of Neoplatonism, in order to indicate knowledge that derives from mystical experience. This had been the meaning of the term "theosophy" for many centuries.

Today, however, "theosophy" refers to the movement created in the last century by a Russian woman, Helena Petrovna Blavatsky (1831-1891), a singular character of undeniable depth. Of a noble family, at a very young age she began a long series of trips to the East, especially India and Tibet, where she met the "Masters of Wisdom" and received their teachings. Endowed with exceptional mediumistic and clairvoyant abilities and an equally exceptional spirit of initiative and courage, Blavatsky gathered the teachings of the mysterious masters and presented a spiritual doctrine whose motto is, "*there is no higher religion than truth.*" This is a "secret doctrine" consisting of the teaching that underlies all the great religions, an esoteric teaching that also includes the doctrine of *karma* and *reincarnation*[64] and many elements found in Hindu and Eastern traditions, and in Neoplatonism, gnosticism, Paracelsus, and the Rosicrucians. The objective of theosophical doctrines is to help man to implement his return to The Absolute through practices such as meditation and contemplation, as well as training in justice, love, beauty, true wisdom and brotherhood. The Theosophical Society was founded in New York in 1875 and was very successful, both in the United States and in Europe. In 1879, the group's headquarters was moved to Adyar, India, where it remains today.

Today as then, the aims of the Theosophical Society include:

1) to form a core of the Universal Brotherhood of humanity, without distinction of race, belief, sex, caste and color.
2) to encourage the comparative study of religions, philosophies and sciences.
3) to investigate the unexplained laws of Nature and the latent powers of humanity.[65]

---

[64] The doctrine of reincarnation, which is widely accepted especially in the East, teaches that one does not live only once, but many times; that is, "one takes on new flesh" in order to purify oneself, evolve, and experience for the purpose of inner growth and personal evolution. The different lives would be comparable to the classes at a school, from kindergarten to university. The various incarnations are regulated by karma, which indicates the effect of the actions performed; in Western terms, this is the law of cause and effect.

[65] *For further reference, see* https://www.theosociety.org/pasadena/ts/tsobject.htm.

The Theosophical Society has no dogmas and does not ask anyone to renounce their religion or affiliation; instead, it asks everyone to show the same respect for the religion of others as is due to their own.[66] All these concepts were very close to the thought of Roberto Assagioli, who believed in the existence of the "Masters." In the essay quoted above, "The Universal Messianic Expectancy," he writes,

> In each age and to each race have appeared men of exceptional high spirituality: founders of religions, sages, teachers, prophets . . . One has merely to recall Confucius and Lao-Tze in China; Buddha in India; Zoroaster in Persia; Solon, Plato and Pythagoras in Greece; Moses, Isaiah, Jesus, Muhammad and, among the moderns, Baha-u-llah, Ramakrisna, Vivekananda, Gandhi, Aurobindo. According to esoteric traditions, in addition to these Beings[67] on the public stage, there exists an Order, a Hierarchy, a Brotherhood of Initiates, called variously Rishis, Mahatmas, Masters, who live unknown and ignored, 'behind the world scene,' but who gather and train disciples and who, *incognito*, beneficently intervene, unknown, in human events with beneficial intentions.

It is precisely with these secret Masters that Madame Blavatsky would have made contact.

From Dr. Eduardo Bratina of Trieste, president of the Italian Theosophical Society, who knew Roberto Assagioli very well, I learned that in the 1920s he attended meetings of the theosophical group of Florence, and that when he moved to Rome his home was used as the meeting place for theosophists residing in the capital. Assagioli also wrote many articles for the magazine *Ultra*, an organ of the independent theosophical group in Rome.[68]

When the Italian Theosophical Society was to be dissolved by the authorities in 1939 because it opposed the government's racial policy,[69] Assagioli resigned to avoid creating problems [for the Society], using these words: "I resign because I

---

[66] For a more in-depth treatment of this topic and of theosophy in general, see *H.P. Blavatsky e la Società Teosofica* [*H.P. Blavatsky and the Theosophical Society*], by Paola Giovetti: Mediterranean Editions, Rome 1991.

[67] *We note that Assagioli does not mention, among these great Beings, the Christ, of whom he evidently had an even higher concept. But the name "Jesus" is included among the "great men," as is quoted here, and the balance of Assagioli's essay clearly indicates that "Christ" (which is not identical with Jesus) is one name for the focus of the "universal messianic expectancy." —Ed.*

[68] *Assagioli's first article for Ultra was published in 1920. An article written by his future wife, Nella Ciapetti, appeared in Ultra in 1919. —Ed.*

[69] *After allying with Nazi Germany, in 1938 the Italian fascist government passed a series of "racial" laws that enforced discrimination and segregation, mostly against Italian Jews and the African inhabitants of the Italian Empire. —Ed.*

THE YEARS OF MATURITY

am Jewish." The Society was dissolved in any event, and the members who objected had various troubles with the political police.[70]

During the war Roberto Assagioli also had many difficulties, but at the end of the conflict he resumed his activities, including the theosophical ones. In May 1946 he commemorated Helena Petrovna Blavatsky with an article published in the magazine of the Theosophical Society, from which I quote some significant passages concerning the work of the founder of the theosophical movement and the figure of the Masters of wisdom:

> One of the brightest gems contained in the spiritual treasure that has been bestowed upon us thanks to the self-denial of H. P. Blavatsky and her early collaborators, is the revelation of the existence of the Masters of Wisdom and Compassion, the Mahatmas, and thus the possibility of making them an ideal model to inspire us in our work of inner perfection . . . The Master of Wisdom and Compassion is truly the perfected man, the man who has developed all the elements and all the potential of human nature in a balanced and harmonious way. It is He who has triumphed over the forces of the inner and outer world with the Supreme Power of the Spirit, He who has penetrated the mysteries of the visible and the invisible with the illuminated mind, with the inner eye and with intuition. He has developed, enlarged and elevated his love to make it capable of enveloping all creatures . . . What matters in spiritual development is not so much the length of the path that is traveled as the right direction. Ten meters traveled in the right direction are worth more than a kilometer of coming and going. And it is precisely the right direction that is offered to us by the Mahatma, and that can be followed by each of us, regardless of the point along the long evolutionary path on which we are found . . . [71]

As can be seen, Assagioli was particularly concerned with the destinies of humanity and the growth of the individual person, and the theosophical doctrines offered him ideas and stimuli that he considered worthy of the utmost attention. In the letter cited above, Edoardo Bratina also remembers with feeling "the morning meditation break that we did together in a small special room, in front of portraits of the two Mahatmas who supported the Theosophical Society." The two

---

[70] From a letter from Dr. Bratina to the author dated 15 August 1992.

[71] *The author has not provided a source citation for this quotation.* —Ed.

Mahatmas mentioned are the Masters whom Helena P. Blavatsky claimed to have met on her travels in the East.

Roberto Assagioli was also in close contact with Alice Bailey (1880-1949) and her Arcane School. Something should also be said about this English woman and her movement, which was connected with theosophy. Alice Bailey described herself as "an unimportant woman who casually, against her will, was forced by circumstances to take on certain tasks for reasons of conscience, knowing what the Master wanted for her."

Alice was from an aristocratic English family and was far removed from any esoteric knowledge. She was just 15 years old when, as she relates in her unfinished Biography, she received a visit from a mysterious character dressed in the European style but with a turban. He foretold her future work as the collaborator with a Master — if she wanted to, and if she was able to change her capricious nature. Alice was astonished and never forgot the unknown visitor. Many years later, when she came into contact with the Theosophical Society, she recognized him in the portrait of Koot Humi,[72] one of the Blavatsky's teachers, who was described as "very close to Christ, dedicated to teaching — an eminent interpreter of the Love-Wisdom that Christ fully expresses."

Alice had a difficult life. While still a young woman she was working in India in social services related to the British army. There she met pastor Walter Evans and married him. The couple settled in the United States, but despite the birth of three girls, the marriage proved disastrous due to Evans' neurotic and despotic character, and ended in a divorce. Alice was 35 years old with three young daughters with no means of support. She worked in a sardine factory to make a living.

It was during this time that she met two English women who had been personal disciples of Blavatsky and who introduced her to theosophy. Years of work and study followed: during the day in the factory and with her daughters, at night the theosophical and esoteric readings. Through the American Theosophical Society Alice met Foster Bailey, who had the same interests and who later became her second husband.

In 1919 Alice had the decisive experience of her life, the one foretold when she was 15 years old: the meeting on a telepathic level with The Tibetan, a Master belonging to the *ashram* (that is, the group) of Koot Humi, who asked her if she wanted to collaborate in the drafting of certain books that he wanted to be written for the public. Alice refused several times, then accepted on a trial basis: it was after writing the first chapter of what later became *Initiation, Human and Solar* that

---

[72] *Sometimes spelled "Kuthumi" by others.* —Ed.

she made herself totally available to the Tibetan, who inspired many texts for a period of thirty years. I quote some titles that are available from the vast catalog:[73] *Destiny of the Nations, Discipleship in the New Age, Letters on Occult Meditation, A Treatise on the Seven Rays*, and many others. The texts deal with the principles of "eternal wisdom," meditation, service as the principle of life, and discipleship; that is, service to humanity and the planet in the approaching New Age.[74]

In 1923 Alice Bailey, together with her husband, created the *Arcane School* for the dissemination of these teachings and for the preparation for new consciousness through the teaching of meditation, a fundamental tool for people to use for freeing personal resources and to heal the split between personality and soul. The School is still operating.[75]

We know that Roberto Assagioli personally met Alice Bailey on several occasions, for example at the conferences at Ascona in Switzerland.[76] He read and appreciated the Tibetan texts and followed the activity of the Arcane School. It also seems that some passages of one of the volumes of the Treatise on the Seven Rays concern him personally, but this has not been conclusively demonstrated.[77]

It is certain that Assagioli's work, which can almost be described as missionary work, his striving for a better humanity, his trust in man and his potential, and his vast conception of the psyche all harmonized well with the basic concepts of Theosophy and the Arcane School.

This passage, taken from *The Destiny of the Nations* by Alice Bailey, could certainly have been by Assagioli, indeed it could have been written by him personally:

> The future will see right relationships, true communion, a sharing of all things . . . and goodwill; we will also have a picture of the future of humanity

---

[73] *All the texts by Alice Bailey are available through Lucis Trust.* —Ed.

[74] *Among the titles of these books is* Esoteric Psychology *(in two volumes), which was probably of particular interest to Roberto Assagioli.* —Ed.

[75] *In Europe, the headquarters are in Switzerland, in Geneva, Rue du Stand 40. The Arcane School is a division of Lucis Trust, headquartered at 866 United Nations Plaza, New York, N.Y. USA* —Ed.

[76] *Both Assagioli and Bailey were teachers and speakers at these conferences (see Assagioli Archive Doc. #21030), which was under the auspices of the International Center for Spiritual Research, a joint venture of Alice Bailey and Olga Fröbe-Kapteyn, at whose property the meetings took place. After Fröbe-Kapteyn severed connections with Bailey at the urging of C.G. Jung in 1933, Ascona became the home of the Eranos Foundation, devoted to the work of Jung.* —Ed.

[77] *Numerous studies since the original publication of this book have confirmed that Assagioli was personally involved and was mentioned in some of the books by Alice A. Bailey, specifically Discipleship in the New Age, and perhaps others as well. Members of the Bailey group who were involved with the Tibetan readings were referred to by initials that were indicative of certain spiritual goals pertinent to them. Assagioli was referred to in some of the books as "FCD," initials which had a spiritual significance to him.* —Ed.

when all nations are united by complete understanding and the diversity of languages — symbolic of differing traditions, cultures, civilizations and points of view — will provide no barrier to right human relations relationships.[78]

Roberto Assagioli was certainly an "esotericist," for he drew many ideas from the doctrinal heritage of the East, he practiced meditation personally and used it as a basic technique of his psychosynthesis. But he filtered everything through his own Western sensitivity, and as a scientist he framed everything into an organic system, perfectly readable and acceptable even by those who have no relationship with esotericism. A biography of Roberto Assagioli would not be complete if it did not take due account of these aspects.

THE INSTITUTE OF CULTURE AND PSYCHIC THERAPY

In 1926 Assagioli founded the *Institute of Culture and Psychic Therapy* in Rome, the purpose of which, according to Article 2 of its Charter, was "to contribute to the physical, moral and spiritual renewal of the individual and the [human] race, promoting a better and a more effective understanding of inner energies and carrying out a work of prevention and psychic cure against the evils that threaten physical and moral health."

At the inaugural session of the Institute, held on May 4th, Assagioli, who held the position of Director (the chairman was Gabriella Rasponi Spalletti [79]), gave a presentation on the topic "How to Educate the Will," a subject that was always very dear to him, and to which he devoted an entire book, *The Act of Will*, many years later.

The program of the Institute was the one already envisaged in *psychagogy*: only in 1933 in fact did the center assume the name of "Institute of Psychosynthesis." As will be recalled, Roberto Assagioli had been developing his thoughts in a complete manner since his youth: the articles on psychology, in which the whole psychosynthetic process is already clear, date back to 1909, when Assagioli was just 21 years old.

The Rome Institute, as Alfredo Scanzani rightly pointed out in an article published in *La Nazione* [*The Nation*] on December 24, 1983, ten years after Assagioli's

---

[78] *This quotation is taken directly from the original English edition of Lucis Publishing Co. New York. —Ed.*

[79] *Countess Gabriella Rasponi Spalletti (1853-1931) was an Italian feminist, educator and philanthropist. She was founder and president of the National Council of Italian Women and was a board member of the Italian Red Cross. She hosted a salon in Rome that attracted writers, philosophers, journalists and politicians. —Ed.*

death, can be considered "a progenitor of those growth centers that became fashionable in the seventies in America and then with us." Assagioli certainly saw individual patients there, and we know that he was very successful as a "doctor of the soul," but he also cared about groups, and he was a pioneer in this respect. Assagioli addressed the psyche of those who were ill (he was a psychiatrist, and this was his specific work), but above all he focused on the healthy psyche, on the positive potential of the human being, and looked for the best ways to bring it out. The ultimate aim — and this was the goal of Assagioli's entire life and work — was to transform the individual, or rather to help him to transform himself, and through the individual to create a future society. This goal was already present in his heart and his mind: a world in which people are conscious and responsible, capable of exercising the will (understood in the highest and most noble sense of the term), able to stimulate their creativity for daily life, and also to emerge from the times of crisis that so often have devastating effects, eager to live in harmony with themselves and with others.

Assagioli called for the exploration of the higher human faculties. He wanted to educate people in self-training: projects which were unusual and innovative for those times.

After all, Assagioli always was a unique character, altogether alone in the dominant cultural landscape. He practiced privately, more inclined to meet with individuals or in daily meetings with small groups than seeking wider acclaim and more prestigious roles. He did not want to belong to static institutions which were typical of the old way of thinking. He often repeated a saying of the German philosopher Hermann Keyserling, who was a close friend: "Whoever deals with the creation of the future cannot pay attention to the quarrels of the present." I also found this phrase among the handwritten notes kept in the Florence archive.

One of the things he cared about most was making himself understood by everyone: from the specialist to the seamstress, everyone had to be able to understand his message. And so it was until the end. His language is in fact clear, simple, and free of any intellectual or didactic conceit. Assagioli had the vocation of the teacher, or rather of the educator — but of an educator devoid of conceit and any sense of superiority; more a traveling companion than a superior.

If in his lectures and in his talks we often find the same concepts repeated with ever new language, presented from different angles, it was certainly not for lack of arguments, but for the deeply felt need to make himself well understood. For this reason he returned to certain premises which he deemed indispensable, and he reiterated certain concepts and ideas.

He was endowed with infinite tolerance, the ability to accept the other, and with humor. He did not judge, and he stimulated human sympathy and joy of life — characteristics that neither the years nor pains and difficulties would ever take away from him.

To get an idea of what Assagioli was like in those years, I repeat the words of Ms. Luisa Lunelli, who knew Assagioli as a doctor and later became a close friend of the whole family. Ms. Lunelli, whom I met in Bologna where she settled in 1990 after staying in America for many years, told me that she had sought the "doctor who worked miracles" (this was the fame enjoyed by Roberto Assagioli at Rome for the successes he had with his patients) as she was tired and depressed after breast-feeding her first child. "I wanted to become his patient," she told me. "Instead, I was healed through friendship with him and with his wife Nella, by the serenity that he always radiated, even in the most difficult times."

Ms. Lunelli's description appears in a short but valuable essay published by the *Centro Studi di Psicosintesi "R. Assagioli"* of Florence, created and directed by Dr. Piero Ferrucci, one of the students closest to Assagioli in his last years of life, entitled *Roberto, Nella and Luisa*.[80] I will draw on it again throughout this biography.

Here, then, was the first meeting between Luisa Lunelli and Roberto Assagioli.

In the mid-1930s, on a sunny June afternoon, I got off the bus in Via Nomentana on the corner with Via Antonio Bosio. Dr. Assagioli, the doctor who "worked miracles," as people called him, lived in Rome, at Via Bosio. I had an appointment with him.

The boundary wall of Villa Torlonia, where the Mussolini family lived, runs along Via Bosio and their surname brought to my mind the farm we had in Romagna, bordering on a property of the Mussolini family. The vision of that beautiful countryside, open to the air and light of the Rabbi River valley, came to mind and eased the tension of my first meeting with a psychiatrist. At that moment, in fact, I didn't even know how I would succeed in describing the case I wanted to present to him, for it was not clear even to myself.

The door of the building at No. 30 was open. I went in and went up a few steps and found myself at the entrance of the Assagioli apartment, a vast room whose singular brightness I noticed. A whiter, thinner, brighter light

---

[80] *An English translation of this essay is available online at https://kennethsorensen.dk/en/?s=Roberto%2C+Nella&id=10440. —Ed.*

than the bright summer sun of Rome. A light that I have not forgotten and that I have only encountered few times in my life.

In the opposite room a middle-aged gentleman finished speaking to an attentive audience. I thought there had been a mistake in the appointment, that I had had an appointment for a lesson, rather than a professional consultation. The teacher came out of the classroom and everyone came around him. Most of them wanted to talk to him. Of course, this was not the time to present my affairs. However, it happened that I found myself next to him and it also happened that he turned to me and said, "Go upstairs," pointing to an internal staircase. "My wife is upstairs and I will be able to talk to you there, if you want." Upstairs I found Mrs. Assagioli with some friends and I sat down with them, and accepted a cup of tea.

Later the doctor also went up. He looked tired and it was evident that he was looking for relaxation. He appreciated the cup of tea that his wife handed him and took part in the playful conversation that was taking place. Again, there was no need to mention my problem. When I started to leave, Assagioli said, "Come back, or rather come back soon. On our shelves you will find something good to read; take what you want. You will certainly find what interests you."

I did return. I went to the shelves and found books and handouts that were interesting. Of course, some were even a little strange; strange things, but good things. So I went back to take new things to read, with some regularity. But soon Signora Assagioli told me that in the next few days they would leave for the countryside, so the house in Rome would be closed. "We always welcome visits in Tuscany," she also said, and I promised her a visit. So it was that I was not a patient of Assagioli that day, nor was I ever. That day, however, a friendship was born that was very long and very good and beautiful.

Evidently Assagioli had understood from the first moment that Luisa Lunelli above all needed friendship, acceptance, positive and stimulating readings, the opening of new horizons: the doctor who "worked miracles" had a great intuition and even on that occasion he was right.

The conference to which Ms. Lunelli refers was probably an esoteric meeting. Assagioli kept his psychiatric activity distinct from his personal interests. The Institute of Culture and Psychic Therapy was located in Via Marsala, while we know from numerous testimonies that meetings with theosophical and esoteric groups took place in his home. Nella Ciapetti, Roberto Assagioli's wife, shared, at least in part, these interests and often participated in the meetings herself.

ROBERTO ASSAGIOLI

The years between 1926 and the immediate pre-war period, when Assagioli had to close the Institute (which in the meantime had become the Institute of Psychosynthesis) for political and "racial" reasons, were very active. In addition to psychiatric, psychological and esoteric work, Assagioli traveled a lot, both in Europe and in the United States, to meet scholars and make psychosynthesis known. And it was in America that psychosynthesis received its first important recognition: we have seen that Roberto Assagioli wrote some of his works in English, precisely for the American groups.

Assagioli was in contact by letters and in person with the most important exponents of the cultural world of his time. We have already mentioned Freud, Jung, Martin Buber and Herman Keyserling.[81] Assagioli also met, among others, Einstein, the writer James Joyce, the Zen master Suzuki, the poet Tagore, the anthropologist Alexandra David-Néel,[82] Lama Govinda,[83] in addition to some of the major exponents of psychology of his time, including Abraham H. Maslow and Michael Murphy,[84] who said of him:

> What Aurobindo calls *yoga,* Maslow *self-actualization* and Fritz Perls *organismic integrity,* Assagioli called *psychosynthesis.* All these share basically the same idea; that there is a natural tendency to evolution, toward unfoldment, that pervades the universe as well as the human sphere, and that our job is to get behind that and make it conscious. But the disciplines that emerge to deal with this unfoldment have to reflect the many-sidedness of the human psyche, and this is why psychosynthesis is so valuable. Assagioli himself was really a man of very wide European culture. He was the truest sage I have ever met.[85]

The publication of two of his basic writings in the prestigious English magazine

---

[81] *Hermann Graf von Keyserling (1880-1946) was a Baltic German philosopher and prolific writer, with whom Assagioli establish a warm relationship and whose work he quoted often. —Ed.*

[82] *Alexandra David-Néel (1868-1969) was a Belgian-French explorer, spiritualist and writer, author of over 30 books, who was famous for her visit to Lhasa, Tibet, when it was forbidden to foreigners. —Ed.*

[83] *Anagarika Govinda (1898-1985) was German-Bolivian (born Ernst Lothar Hoffman) Buddhist who founded the order of Arya Maitreya Mandala and expounded Tibetan Buddhism and meditation. —Ed.*

[84] *Michael Murphy (1930-) is an American who co-founded the Esalen Institute in California. —Ed.*

[85] Quoted in *Roberto Assagioli 1888-1988*, edited by Alessandro Berti and published by the Center for the Studies of Psychosynthesis of Florence, founded and directed by Piero Ferrucci. *This quotation as shown is taken from the original English version: a profile of Michael Murphy in the New Yorker magazine of Jan. 5, 1976, p. 47. See* https://kenneth-sorensen.dk/en/my-personal-experience-with-psychosynthesis/ —Ed.

Hibbert Journal [in 1934 and 1937] contributed greatly to making Assagioli's work known abroad. The first was "Dynamic Psychology and Psychosynthesis," in which Assagioli outlined the history of the psychology of the unconscious, from Janet to Freud, Adler and Jung, including William James' studies on mystical experiences and Keyserling's synthesis of Western and Eastern thought. This article already shows the ovoid representation of the psyche [the so-called "egg diagram"], and the dynamic and self-training aspects of psychosynthesis is presented.

In the second article, "Self-Realization and Psychological Disturbances," Assagioli explored the long and difficult path of those who pursue the awakening of their own spirituality and the search for the meaning of life, and he analyzes the "disturbance" (nights of the soul) that can appear at each stage. Together with problems, Assagioli presents the appropriate therapies to overcome them, and encourages people to undertake this spiritual journey, which is fundamental for the growth of humanity.

These articles were later included as the first two chapters of the book on principles and methods of therapeutic psychosynthesis, published initially in English by the Psychosynthesis Research Foundation of New York in 1965,[86] and translated into Italian by Elena Zanotti in 1973.[87]

THE FAMILY

A lot of love always reigned in the family of Roberto Assagioli, his wife Nella and his son Ilario.

Nella Ciapetti came from a wealthy family; however, it was a wealth based on agriculture, and the family fortunes decreased somewhat with the decline of agricultural incomes. In Capolona, in the Aretino,[88] Nella had a villa surrounded by farms, where the family spent their summer holidays from June to September. Ilario was born there. Nella also owned the apartment in Rome, in Via Bosio. Roberto Assagioli had inherited a house in Chianti from his father, but it was sold when their economic situation became precarious after the war. Overall, there was not much money circulating in the Assagioli household, but there were never financial worries.

---

[86] *Psychosynthesis: A Manual of Principles and Techniques*, Hobbs, Dorman & Co. New York, 1965.

[87] Astrolabio Publishing House, Rome, 1973.

[88] *Capolona is on a series of hills in the province of Arezzo in Tuscany, about 230 km (143 miles) north of Rome and about 90 km (56 miles) south of Florence. Its elevation is about 213 m (700 feet) higher than Assagioli's home in Florence, so the summer climate is cooler and drier.* —Ed.

Ms. Luisa Lunelli told me that Nella Ciapetti was considered a difficult woman by some people, but her goodness was beyond question. She had many responsibilities: it was up to her to manage the family economic situation, deal with the tenants, and manage the farm, so on occasion she had to know how to be very determined and even tough. With her husband, she imposed herself only when it concerned his health. Roberto was always of a delicate constitution: he easily caught flu and bronchitis, and in addition he had suffered from tuberculous synovitis[89] in one knee, so he had to take care of himself and she had to be firm with him. "Roberto worked a lot and sometimes he neglected himself," Luisa Lunelli told me, "and for this reason Nella was sometimes worried. For the rest, she did not take a leading role; there was a lot of understanding and they loved each other very much."

"It was an excellent marriage," said Donatella Ciapetti of Florence, daughter of Nella's brother who lived with her aunt and uncle for years. "They were old and I heard them in the room playing like children, laughing and joking. They were very close and both had a great willingness to let the other do what they wanted. My uncle had his own schedule and slept with a mask over his eyes and wax in his ears, because she moved a lot at night. They didn't bother each other."

Donatella Ciapetti also said that Roberto had met Nella as a patient: she had been very much in love with another man and had fallen into depression. Her husband continued to look after her throughout her life, because Nella was somewhat temperamental and he always protected her and gave her moral support. "The atmosphere of the house was peaceful," says Donatella Ciapetti. "They seemed to be in another world: peace and serenity!"

Roberto Assagioli had a character that everyone describes as incomparable. Ms. Angela La Sala Batà of Rome, who knew and had visited the founder of psychosynthesis since she was a young girl and considered herself his student, referred to him as "simple, modest, humorous — he had a deep serenity. He did not allow his great learning to impose on anyone. Love and harmony were the keynotes — just being close to him was enough to feel better." Angela's mother had an esoteric circle that Assagioli attended and continued to attend even after the war, when he returned to Florence; he went often to Rome to meet friends and hold conferences and meetings, which took place in the home of Ms. La Sala Batà.

---

[89] *Tuberculous (TB) synovitis (a.k.a. Tuberculosis tenosynovitis) is a rare, treatable, but potentially lethal form of extrapulmonary TB. It usually causes chronic inflammation of the tendon and if untreated can progress to severe arthritis, etc.—Ed.*

"Their relationship was of the very best," wrote Luisa Lunelli in her essay, referring to Roberto and Nella Assagioli. "They were different, yes, but complementary, and communication between them was easy . . ." And she adds these intimate and moving notes:

> Their long married love retained youthful hues. After Nella had put on an elegant dress for a show or reception and I, who was helping her get ready, had put her lace gloves and the perfumed handkerchief into her purse, Roberto would enter the room. He came to choose the jewelry to complement the dress. From the jewelry box he would choose a bracelet with turquoise and a ring with a large, rare turquoise, if the dress was green. If the dress was blue, the lapis lazuli necklace and pendant earrings would match. In other cases there was the double necklace of large garnets, which came from an aristocratic grandmother; there was also an oriental pearl necklace and earrings. In short, there was a choice not of great value, but of good taste and careful workmanship. Roberto fastened the necklace to his wife's neck, slipped the ring on her finger, handed her the earrings so that she herself would find the small hole in her earlobe. After making the last gesture, he took a few steps back to observe the details and the whole. He looked at Nella with a look that showed the satisfaction of a husband who presents himself with a beautiful wife to friends. Nella was very beautiful. Then I mischievously asked, "Roberto, when will the second honeymoon happen?" He promptly replied, "We will get it on the schedule soon!"

Nella had confided to Luisa Lunelli that she had given up on marriage because she was no longer very young, but then she had met Roberto and immediately said "yes!" *Roberto was not like any of the others.* "Roberto was a very good man," remembers Luisa Lunelli.

> His goodness was there at every hour of the day. He was ready for any act of service, and didn't ask for anything for himself that wasn't absolutely essential. He treated his family, distant relatives, friends, students, his patients, servants with the same courtesy. He was the head of the family, but it didn't weigh on him. Only when necessary did he assume the appropriate responsibility with strength and clarity of mind. He was interested in his son, his nieces and their friends. He loved their amusements and accepted bets and jokes from them.

He was always ready to help them in their studies. In conversation in the family, however, he never introduced subjects that would display his intellectual superiority. It was years before I realized the extent of his vast literary, historical, scientific and musical learning, the number of modern languages he spoke and how many ancient ones he read. Roberto had a humility that always made him respectful of others. I don't ever remember hearing hostile phrases, negative judgments, or even expressions of simple dislike from him. I never saw the least impatience or intolerance in him. The word 'defect' did not exist in his vocabulary. Defects were 'different qualities,' or uncultivated or misused qualities. Yes, I will always remember how nice it was to live with him, to live by his side. There was a peace that did good and encouraged good. He 'healed' people who were close to him without sessions, without medicines ....

As the reader will remember, Luisa Lunelli had personally experienced this particular type of healing. From these and other testimonies that will be reported later, it is evident that Roberto Assagioli was truly the living expression of his psychosynthesis.

Roberto and Nella's only son, Francesco Ilario, was born in 1923. Ilario was baptized because Nella was Catholic and Assagioli believed that it was up to the mother to give the first religious education to the children. The boy soon revealed himself to be special: intelligent, precociously mature, endowed with a great intellectual curiosity and an innate spirituality. Ilario attended Montessori elementary schools in Rome and then the *Giulio Cesare* [Julius Caesar] high school. At university he chose medicine and then letters, with the intention of helping his father and following in his footsteps. He had inherited a lot from his father, and there was always total understanding and interest between them.

During his adolescence, around the age of fifteen, Ilario fell ill with tuberculosis. He was treated in every way, spent long periods in the sanatorium, but nothing could be done. He died in 1951, just 28 years old. His family, at that time, had already returned to Florence. It was a peaceful death: Ilario knew it was coming; he had accepted his destiny and with his father's help he had prepared himself spiritually for the big step.

Roberto and Nella's suffering over their son's illness was enormous, and the boy realized it. Luisa Lunelli writes:

Ilario, sensitive to his parents' pain, and for their sake, underwent long and painful surgeries without complaint. Although I did not follow his situation closely, I twice saw him experience a collapsed lung. The treatment was useless, so eventually the motor nerve was cut and the diseased lung was permanently immobilized . . . Roberto, despite having entrusted his son to the best Italian and Swiss specialists, followed the medical research carefully and any new medicine or new method that seemed to give confidence was immediately attempted . . . During the better intervals Ilario took the courses at the classical Lyceum. Most of the time, however, he was forced to remain absent. His classmates kept him informed day by day. Ilario studied in bed or in the deck chair; he showed up for exams and always passed them, so he got his classical diploma and enrolled in medicine at the university. . .

Over time, Luisa Lunelli says, the visits of schoolmates became less frequent because at that time the only prevention against tuberculosis was to avoid contact with those who had it. "But during his isolation," we read again in Ms. Lunelli's account, "Ilario had made contact with other friends: friends for whom there was no fear of contagion, great friends, of inner affinity . . ."

For years Ilario read the works of the great philosophers, writers, poets, reaping the most wonderful fruits. He made a collection of maxims that were published privately with the title *From Pain to Peace.* The choice testifies to the young man's spiritual asceticism. In his preface he explained under what conditions and with what intent he had accomplished that long, precious, illuminating work:

When, during long years of illness, I discovered in my numerous readings some maxim, aphorism or thought, I transcribed them to form a collection; I did not think that the time would come when it would be published as a book. It was my keen desire to make them known, since I knew from personal experience how much certain statements about joy, optimism, and hope in the dark moments of life can raise one up and help. The human value of this volume is made clear, in addition to the content, by the fact that it is the result of real suffering — and that the first to have benefitted from its pages is the compiler himself . . .

His father, who had vast literary learning, procured books for his son, stood by his side with his affectionate, serene, available presence, and tacitly made him feel his love.

In the years immediately preceding the war and during the war itself, Ilario's health suffered ups and downs, making his parents hope and despair.

After the war, probably also due to the strains faced in the period in which he remained hidden in the mountains with his father, Ilario got worse and died despite the arrival of penicillin: his body was no longer able to respond. But we will return later to Ilario's death and on what it meant for his parents. Let us now resume the story of Roberto Assagioli's life in the difficult years of the Second World War.

THE SECOND WORLD WAR. *FREEDOM IN JAIL*

Even before the outbreak of the Second World War Roberto Assagioli was accused of "pacifist activity." It was never known precisely who made the accusations, but it can be assumed that his being Jewish was the cause. This is revealed to us by Ms. Luisa Lunelli, who in her aforementioned essay tells how Assagioli had refused to sign [the document] for "the Jerusalem capital," as other Jews in Rome did: it was a practice [of some Jews] to support the war, which in case of victory would give them Zion, that is, Jerusalem.[90]

The problems started in 1936, when Assagioli's international contacts and humanitarian and spiritual activities aroused the suspicions of the fascist regime, which made the work of the Institute [of Psychosynthesis] increasingly difficult until it was closed in 1938. In that same year, it must be recalled, Sigmund Freud also had to leave Vienna and all the psychoanalytic organizations suffered a setback. Roberto Assagioli and his family retired to live in the countryside, where he spent the years of conflict amid many difficulties.

In 1940, accused of pacifism, he had to spend a month in prison. He was arrested at his home in Chianti and taken to Rome, where he remained confined in the Regina Coeli Prison[91] for the entire sweltering month of August. He approached this experience with great courage, indeed transforming it into an opportunity for learning and growth.

---

[90] *At least until the promulgation of the 1938 "racial" laws, a number of Italian Jews were sympathetic to the Fascist regime and occupied significant offices and positions in politics and economy. Italy supported Zionism to some extent; by helping the Zionist cause, Mussolini hoped to gain influence in the Middle East at the expense of the British Empire. Some Italian Jews circulated a "Jerusalem Letter" in support of the regime in return for a promise that they would be given Jerusalem if Italy achieved its aims in the Middle East. —Ed.*

[91] *The Regina Coeli [Queen of Heaven] Prison in Rome was a Catholic convent built in 1654 and converted to a prison in 1881. During the Fascist regime it served for the detention of political prisoners. —Ed.*

In his unfinished autobiography Assagioli makes a brief mention of that period:

> . . .It was only one month and, under my circumstances, nothing heroic, and nothing at all compared with Frankl[92] or anything of that kind. But I was in jail, and I didn't know how long it would last and what would be the outcome.
>
> Anyhow, I had one of the happiest periods of my life. I could meditate as much as I wanted with a free conscience. I went at it, and, as I was considered dangerous and infecting others, I was put in a separate room. Before trial one could have a room where one was safe, and order food, so no physical suffering, only the confinement. But it was for me a cell. Then I discovered that the chaplain had a copy of Dante's *Divine Comedy*, so I carefully re-read the *Paradise*. You can imagine how I enjoyed it.
>
> It's nothing dramatic, but it might interest people who have been or are going to jail — how to make the best of it.

It is worth dwelling a little on Assagioli's way of living in prison, because it is an experience that says much about his character, and about which we have two first-hand accounts: one from Ms. Lunelli and one by Assagioli himself — and it is an authentic rarity, since Assagioli rarely spoke about himself, and wrote about himself even less.

So here is the account of Luisa Lunelli, who incidentally found herself in the Assagioli home when his arrest had taken place and was able to comfort Nella and help her through those difficult days. "I saw Roberto a few months later," she writes,

> and of course I asked about that August in the Regina Coeli. Well . . . he seemed to have forgotten it! He thought it over and then agreeably replied, "Yes, it was not comfortable, there were inconveniences, but it was a very interesting and useful time." He had had the opportunity to contact a type of people who are difficult to meet. The investigators had to know his ideas, so he had the opportunity to talk about psychosynthesis. They listened to him

---

[92] Viktor Frankl (1905-1997), Viennese Jewish psychiatrist and neurologist, creator of logotherapy. He survived three concentration camps, but lost his young wife, parents, a brother, and many friends and colleagues. He wrote the best-selling book *Man's Search for Meaning* [originally titled *A Psychologist Experiences the Concentration Camp* in German] about that dramatic experience. For more information see Paola Giovetti, *Viktor Frankl, Vita e opere del fondatore della logoterapia* [*Life and works of the Founder of Logotherapy*], Edizioni Mediterranee, Rome, 2001. —*Additional Notes by Editor.*

carefully. Eventually he was told that his ideas were "interesting." Roberto was happy. In fact it was one of the first recognitions of psychosynthesis!

He emphasized the importance of having hours and days available for a rereading of the *Divine Comedy* and some minor works. His in-depth knowledge of Dante and the perfect symbols with which the poet expressed his experience had given Assagioli excellent material for exercises in spiritual psychosynthesis.

The days in prison eventually became exercises in "personal psychosynthesis," even though they were involuntary. The distribution of food when you are hungry and waiting for it evokes thanks, even if unspoken, to those who cooked it and those who offer it to you. Roberto recalled that thoughts of gratitude towards the animal that had provided it, with the sacrifice of its own life — something that should always be done when eating meat — met no objection from even the roughest prisoners.

Serenely he smiled, remembering the "uncomfortable" situation. His description was very different from what I would have had from any other person who was in the same situation. I realized that during that month he had lived in a courageous collaboration with the inevitable. But there is more: *Roberto had not uttered a single bitter word against anyone.*

Let's now see Assagioli's own reflections on his prison experience. It is a text that was written out of inner need and also at the request of friends, but which in reality remained a sketch and was never published.[93] It is located in the notes of the Florence archive. Immediately at the beginning Assagioli explains what his concept of peace is:

Everyone has an ideal of peace. Nobody wants war for its own sake. But as a psychologist, I don't believe that peace can be secured by merely political and legal means, such as treaties, leagues, pacts, etc., and even less by a systematic and violent opposition to war, by "making war on war." Consequently, I am not and never have been a "pacifist" in the current militant and even ideological sense. I am deeply convinced that peace is fundamentally a psychological problem. I believe that there is in man a fundamental fighting instinct or tendency, deeply rooted in his animal nature . . . I believe in first educating an

---

[93] Assagioli's notes have been gathered by Catherine Ann Lombard and published in English in 2016 as Freedom in Jail. *The quotations here and below are taken from that source and match the original notes in the Archive, which are in English.* —Ed.

élite of men and women in these principles, in applying and solving the problem [of peace] in ourselves and in our immediate surroundings, in becoming living examples of *realized peace* in ourselves, in our families, in our work; in demonstrating the possibility of right and harmonious relations . . . It is a slow process, but in my opinion the only sure [one] in the long run.

The basic concepts of Roberto Assagioli recur: the ongoing education of the human being, the need for inner growth, the evolution of the individual. Only in this way can society change and become better. But let's see how Assagioli continues with his story, which is mainly psychological and goes beyond his personal experience, becoming a real lesson in knowing how to live. As a preface we read:

I have been in much doubt whether to write down and publish this "prison diary" or not. First of all, my little adventure was not heroic or even dramatic in any way. A month's imprisonment without any physical hardships or sufferings is in itself a trifling uninteresting incident when compared with the tragic . . . happenings, the heroic deeds, the terrible sufferings of countless actors of the World War. Then I feel a strong reluctance to draw the public attention upon my personality.
On the other hand:
1) I felt a strong and spontaneous urge to write down my experience when I was still in jail.
2) Biographies and autobiographies have a strong, unparalleled educational value, and I remember how much help and inspiration I have derived from many of them. A living example exerts an influence such as no other form of teaching . . . can attain. Also they reach a much wider public than merely scientific writings.
3) One of the purposes and uses of this [booklet] is to show (and implicitly teach) how to rise continuously from personal situations, happenings, incidents and experiences to the general problems, to principles and laws of [an] impersonal nature/universal scope; how to use *every* circumstance for constructive ends, for training and developing some part of one's being; how to preserve serenity, how to get out interest, zest, *joy* from *everything*.

Assagioli then goes on to deal with the real theme of his autobiographical text, the one that is most dear to him and is entitled *Freedom in Jail*:

I realized that I was *free to take* one or another attitude towards the situation, *to give* one value or another to it, to *utilize* it or not in one or another way.

I could rebel inwardly and curse; or I could submit passively, vegetating; or I could indulge in the unwholesome pleasure of self-pity and assume the martyr's role; or I could take the situation in a sporting way and with a sense of humor, considering it as a novel and interesting experience (what the Germans call an *Erlebnis*) [an experience]. I could make of it a rest cure; or a period of intense thinking either about personal matters, reviewing my past life and pondering on it, or about scientific and philosophical problems; or I could take advantage of the condition in order to submit myself to a definite training of my psychological faculties to make psychological experiments upon myself; or finally as a spiritual retreat.

I had the clear sure perception that this was entirely my own affair; that I was *free to choose* any or several of these attitudes and activities; that this choice would have definite and unavoidable effects which I could foresee and of which I was fully *responsible*. There was no doubt in my mind about this essential *freedom* and *power* and their inherent privileges and responsibilities. A responsibility towards myself, towards my fellow mankind and towards life itself or God.

Assagioli explains what the term "acceptance" authentically means, and he considers its "positive and manly" aspect. He writes this:

Not a passive, sad "resignation," but a positive/serene acceptance of an unavoidable condition, an elimination of all useless emotional reactions and rebellion — an active search for the best way of utilizing in the fullest measure the opportunities offered by the new situation.

It was not difficult for me, for various reasons:

First: I have been for a long time convinced of the stupidity of rebellion against what cannot be changed. If we kick against a wall, it is our feet which suffer!

I knew well that the study of the effects of psychological states upon the body has demonstrated that violent emotions, such as fear and anger, produce real poisons in the body . . . upset the digestion, etc. It would have been foolish indeed on my part if I had aggravated my situation by poisoning my nervous system and straining my liver!

Second: As my vocation and work is that of a psychologist, my life in jail offered me a most interesting, unique/special opportunity for new observations and unusual experiments. It is indeed a great privilege that a psychologist does not need material implements of any kind in order to pursue his research. The painter needs canvas, colors and brushes; the sculptor needs chisel, clay or marble. The chemist and the biologist need laboratories with delicate instruments and all sorts of chemicals and substances. The psychologist too for certain special research . . . needs instruments, etc. But many other studies, experiments, indeed for those which have the most central/highest importance and value, he needs absolutely no material thing.

His self, his body, his surrounding environment, his fellowmen, the universe, in their varied relationships and ceaseless interactions provide a constant and inexhaustible field of observations and of action . . .

In Assagioli's autobiographical writing we find yet another passage on the meaning of *acceptance*. It is appropriate to report it because it contains other ideas on the dynamic interpretation of this attitude, so important in life:

"Accept everything," but then remain passive?? Rebellion — in reality is something that must be rather well understood in order to avoid making mistakes — To accept *spiritually* is *not* to suffer passively. Spiritual acceptance is something *positive, dynamic*. It means not to react emotionally, personally, not "push away" some experience, but to draw the lesson it offers, its gift. For example: something happens that is *unfavorable:* disease, failure, someone's hostilities — difficulties. Our spontaneous, "natural," "human" reaction is to consider the thing as *bad*, as something we rebel against, to oppose, to lament, something for which to seek help against, etc. This is a mistake.

Spiritual attitude: *accept* with benevolence the trial, this "hostile thing." Ask ourselves what its message is. That is, investigate its cause (above all in ourselves) — try to understand its significance — see what function it can have, ask ourselves — "what can I build on top of this?"

Only after this, it may be clear that it is our duty to actively eliminate the cause (*this is not always the case*), but then we do this with a *completely different* temperament. The magic of our attitude — true inner freedom with which we *then* gain freedom and the power to integrate.[94]

---

[94] *Translated from Italian notes by Catherine Ann Lombard in* Freedom In Jail, *op.cit. P. 54.* —Ed.

In this short text, which has remained unfinished and never published,[95] we find several key points of Roberto Assagioli's thought: serenity, a constructive and dynamic attitude, availability to others and to life, and spirituality. We will have the opportunity to explore these aspects in a deeper way later.

We don't know much about the actual period during the war. As has been said, the Assagioli family left Rome and moved to the countryside, first to Roberto's house in Chianti, then to Nella's house in Capolona near Arezzo. It is known that Roberto spent several periods "in hiding" in the house of his wife's pastor, who was certainly a safe and faithful person. This period of isolation had become necessary, explained Ms. Lunelli in her essay, not only because he was a Jew. He belonged to a "mixed" family (his wife and son were baptized), and therefore Roberto was a "discriminated Jew."[96] There had been interrogations, but in the end his case was "filed" by the fascist police.

The greater danger, especially in the last years of the conflict, came from being considered wealthy, even if in reality the family was well-off, but certainly not rich. In addition, the villa at Capolona was isolated and surrounded by a large park, and the risk of blackmail and extortion was serious. Hence the decision to hide, at least for a time, with serious discomfort for Roberto's always fragile health and especially for that of Ilario, who spent long periods with his father. The strains contributed to further undermine his health, which was already attacked by tuberculosis.

THE RESUMPTION OF WORK

In September 1944, before the war was ended, Roberto Assagioli began to think about reconstruction and the resumption of cultural activities. Showing great optimism and boundless trust in mankind, he wrote a circular letter to his friends (including C.G. Jung) in which he talks about the years of forced hiding, past and unfinished difficulties, and his great desire to be together with them in peace, harmony and goodwill. Here is the text of the letter, a copy of which is kept at the ETH-Bibliotek, Wissenschaftliche Sammlungen, in Zurich:

---

[95] *It had not been published at the time of this writing, but* Freedom in Jail *was edited by Catherine Ann Lombard and published by Edizione Istituto di Psicosintesi in Florence in 2016.—Ed.*

[96] *The category of "discriminated Jews" was established as an exception within the broader "racial" laws of the Italian fascist regime. This status offered some degree of protection, but it did not completely shield individuals from persecution. —Ed.*

Dear Friends,

Eager to reestablish the good ties that connected us in the past as soon as possible, I thought I'd start by sending you this collective letter, given the practical limitations of the moment. I am happy to be able to tell you that my family and I are alive and free. The Germans and the Fascists did me the honor (if not the pleasure) of seeking me personally; therefore I had to play hide and seek with them for several months in the area of Alpe di Catenaia (in the province of Arezzo) and in the upper Tiber Valley. With the help of God and various good people (local friends, farmers, a paratrooper and various other Englishmen whose fate I shared in part), the searchers always came too late . . . Our home in Nussa, Capolona, was ransacked and then blown up with dynamite. On the cellar floor I found piles of writings and notes in disarray, which represented my work for over 35 years. I have started cleaning them up and putting them in order. We are temporarily housed in the part of the farm that was less damaged by the grenades. We have no news of Villa Serena[97] yet. I'm prepared for the worst because even there I had . . . a bad political reputation. As many of you know, I was arrested in 1940 on an accusation of raising and spreading prayers for peace and other crimes of internationalism.

I am not yet able to make specific plans for the future. When I can, I will make trips to Rome and to Florence. In the first relatively quiet months of "my secret life" (autumn 1943-winter 1944) I worked on revising my writings in Italian so that I could then combine them in two or three volumes, and write a book in English on psychosynthesis. I also wrote an essay on "Politics and Psychology - The Ways of Reconstruction." Now, I have various difficult practical problems to deal with, but I have resumed my spiritual and cultural activities and I intend to intensify them and extend them as I have the opportunity. I feel the inner command — and I respond to it with all of my being — to play my small part in the great and joyful work of individual, national and global renewal. There are wonderful possibilities, which will be implemented if each and every one of us is willing and able to do our part, in harmonious cooperation with people and groups of good will.

---

[97] *Villa Serena was an experiment in community living, a kind of spiritual guest house, initiated by Assagioli. It was located about 22 km (14 miles) from Florence at an altitude of about 900 feet in the hills near the provincial road to Siena. See Assagioli Archives Doc. #8340.* —Ed.

Despite the ongoing difficulties, Roberto Assagioli knew that the worst was past and was preparing for the recovery, inviting all men of good will to participate in the "great and joyful work of renewal." For the resumption of his work Assagioli chose Florence, the city where he had moved at the time of his university studies and where he had completed his education. A house was purchased at number 16 Via San Domenico, the road leading to Fiesole, and here Assagioli established his center of operations. On the ground floor was the headquarters of the Institute with a conference room; their home was on the second floor. Ida Palombi, the faithful and invaluable secretary and assistant who had followed Assagioli from Rome, lived on the third floor for many years. After Roberto's death, she presided over the Institute of Psychosynthesis.

In Florence Assagioli resumed his studies, his private activity as a psychiatrist and psychotherapist, his work for the Institute, and lectures on the topics of psychosynthesis and spirituality. The lectures were very popular, so much so that the room was often insufficient and people had to listen from the vestibule and the stairs. An external microphone was installed so that everyone could hear. The conferences were not for specialists, but were open to anyone who was interested: Assagioli was very keen to bring people from all walks of life together and to be understood by anyone, regardless of their cultural background.

Ms. Tina Muzzi from Florence [later] became a collaborator of Assagioli for a truly innovative humanitarian project, *Il Centro Incontri e Collaborazione* [The Meeting and Collaboration Center], which was the first telephone emergency help center in Italy.[98] She describes Assagioli's conferences:

> Through Dr. Roberto Jacorossi, professor of art history, I was invited to listen to one of the conferences that Assagioli held weekly at the headquarters of the Institute of Psychosynthesis that he had founded. In a plain little room in one of the first houses on the road that goes up to Fiesole, people flocked to listen, fascinated, to an old gentleman who said, with the most natural air in the world, some amazing things that I had not even imagined. His figure was slender, his voice thin, his smile very sweet, and his eyes and words penetrated the soul.

---

[98] The Center was created in 1963 as a branch of an initiative that had arisen years earlier in France by local Psychosynthesis Centers to combat psychological isolation and suicide. Assagioli entrusted the Italian office to Ms. Muzzi, his niece Donatella Ciapetti, and his great friend and collaborator Gabriello Cirenei. The Center offered 24-hour phone support, as well as socializing. It was called "the big family for those who feel alone." It was a secular initiative, which members of various religions (Catholic priests, the chief rabbi of Florence, the evangelical pastor and the Adventist pastor) joined, and which for several years played an important social and humanitarian role. It preceded the various forms of telephone help that we know well today.

We know from numerous testimonies that Assagioli's lectures were highly appreciated, both by simple interested parties and by scholars and specialists. The texts are available [in the Archives at] the Institute: the variety and multiplicity of themes allows us to realize how vast Assagioli's interests were. Ms. Muzzi, who frequented the Assagioli house for a long time, also told of other experiences she had with the founder of psychosynthesis:

> We were introduced by Baroness Zoe Borelli, who combined cultural eclecticism with impressive psychic gifts, and by her husband General Alacevich.[99] After a while we were admitted upstairs where Assagioli's private rooms were. We meditated on the day of the full moon or witnessed experiments to test the extrasensory skills of those present. There were also experiments in telepathy using Rhine cards and psychometrics: Assagioli had previously prepared sealed envelopes marked with a number, which psychics had to hold in their hands while trying to perceive the content.

Ms. Muzzi herself turned out to be a good psychometric subject. In the Assagioli household, the Muzzi couple also participated in mediumistic sessions with a medium in trance who spoke with direct voice. These sessions were more interesting to Nella, Assagioli's wife, and he didn't hinder her. However, he rarely took part personally.

His interest, as Ms. Muzzi pointed out, was above all with the phenomena studied by parapsychology, in the "supernormal" faculties to which he attributed scientific, philosophical and even practical importance, especially for diagnosis and treatment. Assagioli's notes on this topic are kept in the Assagioli Archive, filed under "Parapsychology." The existence of supernormal faculties he considered "scientifically established" thanks to the observations and experiments that had been rigorously documented by Osty,[100] Mackenzie,[101] Servadio [102] and

---

[99] *Zoe Borelli Vranski (1888-1980) was a Croatian artist. She and her husband were jointly the Secretaries of the Italian Society of Metapsychics, which had been founded by Assagioli in 1938 and which later became the Florence branch of the Italian Society of Parapsychology. —Ed.*

[100] *Eugène Osty (1874-1938) was a French physician and psychical researcher, and longtime director of the* Instiut Métaphysique International [International Metaphysical Institute] *in Paris. He wrote several books on paranormal phenomena. —Ed.*

[101] *William Mackenzie (1877-c.1960) was a British biologist and writer who lived in Italy and was associated with the Universities of Turin and Genoa. He joined Assagioli in investigating the "thinking horses" in Germany and was President of the* Italian Society for Parapsychology *and edited the journal* Parapsicologia. *—Ed.*

[102] *Emilio Servadio (1904-1994) was an Italian physician and psychoanalyst who investigated telepathy in connection with his psychoanalytic work and published papers in this connection. —Ed.*

Rhine;[103] and to them he attributed these merits: "Great extension of our knowledge of the breadth and faculty of the human soul; a very effective contribution, perhaps the most powerful, to eradicate materialism; comfort, reawakening of faith for many thousands of people."

After having warned against the dangers that can derive from misguided involvement with these phenomena (credulity, fanaticism, exploitation, quackery etc.), Assagioli calls for a "scientific, serene, impartial, calm, prudent but open investigation" of the phenomena which he defines "supernormal" and concludes, "You cannot ignore them or fight them. [This is a] fascinating trend, an irrepressible need . . . that, if not satisfied by science, will manifest in circuitous ways, without control." Words that are still profoundly true today. [104]

Despite precarious health, Assagioli always traveled a lot, and immediately after the war he resumed his practice of traveling often to meet scholars and to hold and attend conferences. Ms. Angela La Sala Batà of Rome said that after settling in Florence, Assagioli maintained the practice of returning periodically to the capital to give private lectures at the Circle created by his mother. In Florence Assagioli also received many visits from Italian and foreign scholars, poets, writers and artists. Throughout his life, Assagioli was animated by a great intellectual curiosity. His interests were as vast as his love for art in all its expressions, and for the most diverse cultural and humanitarian events. His attitude of extreme helpfulness and amiability towards others did the rest: we will deal with them more in the chapter dedicated to interviews.

PROGRESSIVE JUDAISM

The house in Via San Domenico was also home to a particular initiative by Roberto Assagioli: the Italian Union for Progressive Judaism, which he founded in the early 1950s as a member organization of the World Union for Progressive Judaism. The Union, which advocated an attitude of openness and collaboration towards all

---

[103] *J. B. Rhine (1895-1980) was an American botanist who was instrumental in the founding of parapsychology as a discipline. He founded the parapsychology laboratory at Duke University, as well as* The Journal of Parapsychology *and the* Parapsychological Association, *and wrote several books on parapsychological subjects. —Ed.*

[104] *Assagioli's writings on parapsychology have been gathered by Kenneth Sörensen and published as a free e-book with the title* Psychosynthesis and Parapsychology, *available online at https://kennethsorensen.dk/en/shop-en/. At the same website is a fascinating overview of Assagioli's research in parapsychology by Francesco Baroni, PhD, titled "Roberto Assagioli and Parapsychology."—Ed.*

peoples and religions, was perfectly in line with Assagioli's thought, whose way of being Jewish we have already mentioned.

He had an extremely cordial relationship, based on mutual respect, with Martin Buber, the prophet of liberal and progressive Judaism. The connection dated back to before the war. Assagioli wrote a letter to Martin Buber sent from Rome on June 19, 1946 which was kindly made available to me, together with other letters and articles related to Judaism, by Ms. Manuela Sadum Paggi of Florence. In the letter he wrote, "Many many years ago I had the honor of making your acquaintance in Florence. Since then I have read your writings published in Italian with great admiration. I particularly appreciated your *Seven Talks on Judaism*. In this spirit I wrote an essay entitled "Psychosynthesis of the Jewish People," which I read at the Jewish Circle in Rome last December . . ."[105]

There was a cordial correspondence between Buber and Assagioli, which shows how far Assagioli was involved in the Jewish cause — more precisely, in the cause of progressive, open, liberal Judaism aimed at peace between peoples. Assagioli participated in various international conferences of the Union, spoke on several occasions at the youth camps, and promoted the publication of the Union's *Bulletin*, whose editorial office was also located in his home.

In his article "Progressive Judaism and Psychology" published in issue 3, March 1955 by *La Voce Unione Italiana* [*The Voice of the Italian Union*], Assagioli explains very clearly his relationship with Judaism, and in particular the contribution that Hebrew tradition had made to psychosynthesis:

> . . . In the development of the theory and practice of psychosynthesis I draw inspiration from the Jewish tradition. The basis of the spiritual psychology of which I am an exponent, and towards which various other psychologists have been aiming for some time, is the biblical affirmation that man was made in the image and likeness of God and therefore there is in man an element similar to God. From these bases derives the traditional Jewish teaching of the human psychological constitution composed of three elements: *nephesh, ruah* and *neshamah*.[106] This represents its spiritual aspect. Looking towards the future, progressive Judaism could and should, in my opinion, take on the task of gathering from the long and rich Jewish

---

[105] The conference was repeated at the Jewish Youth Club of Florence.

[106] Translatable in today's terms as instinctual part, consciousness, superconscious.

tradition and the living experience of its mystics and *zaddiks*,[107] the large amount of valuable psychological data that can be found there, using them in combination with the best that modern psychology has to offer. In this way, progressive Judaism would help this new science to overcome the materialistic tendencies and academic timidity that limit its development and prevent the recognition of the superconscious sphere of human nature and the evaluation of its spiritual sphere. In this way psychology will truly become what it can and should be according to its own name: the science of the soul, and will help man develop and use the admirable latent possibilities in his true being for the good of all.

Once again Assagioli expresses his trust in the human being and in the contribution that "the science of the soul" can provide for its enrichment and evolution. Another unpublished article, for which I also owe to the kindness of Ms. Sadom Paggi, is titled "*Shalom*" and explains what the authentic meaning of this term is. The explanation also serves to better illustrate the spirit of progressive Judaism in which Assagioli recognized himself:

> . . . both in the Bible and in much of the latest literature, the word *Shalom* has usually a far bigger and far richer connotation than the word *peace*, as it is ordinarily understood. The root-meaning of the word is that of completeness or soundness, and so it comes to mean the well-being, both physical and spiritual, of the individual and of the community.
>
> In order to realize and express *Shalom* in this deeper and wider meaning, the first step is, of course, a mutual tolerance, which excludes every fanaticism, imposition and aggressiveness. But this is only the first, *elementary* step. It must be followed by the recognition and the positive appreciation of the need and the usefulness of differences.
>
> Unity does not require uniformity. It means an organic wholeness of many different parts. This implies, that wholeness — which is expressed, for instance, as health in the physical body — requires a dynamic equilibrium or creative tension between opposite poles, and the harmonious cooperation of many different organs.
>
> In this way differences are acknowledged and retained while recognizing that they are relative and not mutually exclusive, but are essentially, and

---

[107] A zaddik *was a righteous and saintly person by Jewish standards.* —Ed.

should be practically, subordinated to the higher unity or wholeness; that they have a common origin and serve the same ultimate purpose.

In addition, the term *shalom* understood in the way indicated above provided Assagioli with an original example of his psychosynthesis:

> This conception of *Shalom* has a universal application. The fields in which we are called to demonstrate it are mainly four: first, within ourselves, between the various conscious and unconscious elements of our complex being. Without this inner peace, this "psychosynthesis," we are apt to project our inner conflicts into our relations with our fellowman, or at least we can have only a limited and uncertain effectiveness.
>
> *Shalom* between individuals — first of all in the family, and then in the various complex relationships of social life — requires a true feeling and practice of *brotherhood*, based on mutual understanding, but having its higher source in the realization that we are sons of the One God and therefore are truly brothers.
>
> For the third manifestation of *Shalom*, namely a sure and lasting peace, the nations must be considered, and consider themselves as the organs of a planetary organism — the One Humanity.
>
> The fourth application of *Shalom* is in the religious field where we often find intolerance and narrowness, fanaticism and strife, an outright negation of religion, which essentially means connection and unification between man and God and between man and man.
>
> *Shalom* must be expressed within each religion and, in our case, between the various tendencies existing in Judaism; and it must find expression in the relationships between the various religions of the world, which are historic representations of the one and the same universal truth and have their source in the one true God.
>
> May we succeed in demonstrating peace individually, and may we cooperate to bring about in the world this wholeness and unity — the true *Shalom*.[108]

Truly noble words, which offer an original and admirable synthesis of Assagioli's thought in the psychological, social and religious fields.

---

[108] *These extracts for Assagioli's essay are not translated from the author's Italian text but taken directly from the English-language document titled "Shalom" found in the records of the Psychosynthesis Research Foundation. — Ed.*

ROBERTO ASSAGIOLI

THE DEATH OF ILARIO

In the previous chapter we have already mentioned some details about Ilario, Roberto Assagioli's only son. Ill with tuberculosis since adolescence, Ilario could not take advantage of the antibiotics that came from America at the end of the war: for him it was too late, because his weakened body no longer responded to the drugs.

Having lost hope in medicine, Ilario and his family turned to prayer. Luisa Lunelli, the friend who has already given many accounts of the family life of Roberto Assagioli and his loved ones, recounts in her essay that, being already in contact with Padre Pio,[109] she suggested taking Ilario to the friar, whose repute for holiness was already well known. The idea was welcomed joyfully: Nella was Catholic and Ilario, as you will remember, had been baptized. In addition, the boy was deeply religious and had a great devotion to St. Francis. Padre Pio was Franciscan and stigmatized as the saint had been. Although exhausted from the illness, Ilario was happy when the opportunity presented itself.

The trip and the stay in San Giovanni Rotondo are described by Ms. Lunelli, who accompanied Ilario and his mother:

> The train journey from Arezzo to the village of Gargano was a challenge. Rails, bridges, stations — everything was under construction or under repair. The convoy had to stop continuously to allow workers time to lay or repair a few meters of track. The delay could last for hours. The train resumed its progress, but the engineer had to proceed at a walking pace before finding some safer stretch. Our journey lasted two days. There was no food or drink service on the train. People slept on their feet because there was no place to lie on the floor, or leaned against the walls of the corridor or on a sympathetic traveling companion. Roberto had been able to provide us with a private compartment, but none of the travelers standing in the corridor ever asked to enter: Ilario was always lying down and his white face held them back. The trip, however, did not cause any particular discomfort for Ilario. From Foggia a rickety bus took us to the village of San Giovanni Rotondo in two hours. From the small hospital we could get a wheelchair and so we had transportation for Ilario . . .

---

[109] *Pio of Pietrelcina, born Francesco Forgione (1887 – 1968), widely known as Padre Pio (Italian for 'Father Pius'), was an Italian Capuchin friar. He spent most of his religious life in the convent of San Giovanni Rotondo. He was marked by stigmata in 1918, and was the founder of the Casa Sollievo della Sofferenza, a hospital built near the convent of San Giovanni Rotondo. Many healings have been attributed to him or to his influence. After his death, his devotion continued to spread among believers all over the world. He was beatified in 1999 and canonized in 2002. —Ed.*

Padre Pio celebrated mass at dawn every day and was always awaited by a large crowd who tried to touch him and kiss his hand. He defended himself energetically, but he always looked attentively among the crowd. Ms. Lunelli says, "He saw Ilario's chair and gestured for it to be brought forward. One of his men opened a passage into the crowd and brought it to him. Padre Pio greeted Ilario, and wanted the chair to be taken to the side of the altar while he celebrated mass. And so he had this done every day that we were there."

After mass Padre Pio used to bring some friends into the cloister: during the entire period of his stay in San Giovanni Rotondo, Ilario was always among them. Ilario did not say anything to his mother and friend about his meetings with the *padre*. Nella had hope, says Luisa Lunelli, but perhaps Ilario saw something miraculous in the Friar's attention: "a fatherly encouragement for the departure that was already decided; a tender parting farewell . . ."

Death took Ilario serenely before dawn on November 6, 1951: the boy had asked his father, who was assisting him, for something to eat. Roberto Assagioli had gone to the kitchen to prepare it, but when he returned, Ilario had already closed his eyes forever.

Donatella Ciapetti, Assagioli's niece, was ten years younger than Ilario and was very close to her unfortunate and extraordinary cousin, with whom she had often kept company. She told me, "The night Ilario died I suddenly woke up at four because I felt a presence at the door and then at the head of the bed next to me. I didn't see anyone but the feeling of presence was clear and unmistakable. The next morning they told us that Ilario had died just at four."

Luisa Lunelli did not go to the funeral, but a few days later she visited the Assagioli house. It was a beautiful sunny day, and as Roberto welcomed her she said to him with tears in her eyes, "His eyes no longer see our sun;" to which Roberto had smiled gently and affirmed confidently, "His eyes see quite another Sun today!"

Nella was shocked by the death of Ilario. "Nella did not speak," writes Ms. Lunelli.

> She didn't like visits, she did not want condolences . . . She suffered terribly, and preferred to suffer alone. You could see in her the effort to control herself, and you also could see that it was impossible for her. But Roberto was beside her. United in the same pain, he stood by her side, never leaving her and always keeping silent. He only asked her a few thoughtful questions to inquire about her need, her desire. Nella could accept this

attention. At the same time his silence told her that he understood and respected her — that he respected her, and waited for her. Nella felt the warmth of this expectation, felt the love that radiated from it. Her resistance softened, the light returned, the wound in her heart bled less . . . and slowly Nella, helped by Roberto, was able to recover and return to being the energetic woman she had always been.

These words of Ms. Lunelli allow us to get to know the Assagioli family better, to understand the relationships between father, mother and son, and the quality of their feelings.

But to truly understand Ilario it is essential to read his collection of texts by famous authors, poems, and his spiritual diary. He was certainly a cultured young man with an inclination toward spirituality. The collection *From Pain to Peace* shows the vastness of his readings, ranging from Greek and Latin literature to Eastern philosophy, from the Church Fathers to the mystics of all times and all religions, from the great poets and thinkers of the past to the current ones. Undoubtedly, the influence of his father, a man of profound culture who was open to any contribution of thought, was decisive.

Ilario read and gradually chose the passages that struck him most; over time he created a book divided by themes, a real mine of wisdom and spirituality, and wrote in the preface, "The human value of this volume, in addition to its content, is given by the fact that it is the result of real suffering and that the first to draw help from its pages is the compiler himself. Its immediate purpose is to help one to accept and overcome pain, recognizing its purifying and elevating function . . ."

In his spiritual diary, Ilario explores this concept: "One of the reasons I am happy to have suffered is this: when I try to encourage and comfort someone, I can do it by really understanding his pain and I will not have to keep silent if he says to me: 'But you don't know what it is to suffer.' Instead, I will be able to answer, 'Yes, I do know, and from this I want to help you overcome your pain.'" Pain was therefore accepted as a mission: it is not easy to hear words of this kind coming from a person in his 20s.

Ilario also accepted death: a poem entitled "The Divine Goal," written in February 1951, a few months before he died, proves it.

"Dying
is like leaving
the house
at dawn,"
said
old Chuang-Tze.
It's like quenching your thirst
with fresh dew
on the radiant
meadows of the sky;
feeling
free and light
in the blue
immensity
beyond every shadow
beyond all illusion.
Dying
is stepping out of time,
to enter reality.
Why are you crying, brother?
Why tremble so much?
We leave
the ephemeral
to buy the eternal.
Look up
and we contemplate
the starry sky:
the points of light
are milestones
on the roads of the cosmos,
the supreme Goal
of the human soul:
return to the sublime
Divine Home.

Ilario Assagioli's writings are essentially a search for God, a search that became more intense over time. Shortly before his death the young man remembered the "suggestive and encouraging" words of Muhammad: "God says, 'Whoever draws close to me by a hand's length, I will draw close to him by an arm's length. Whoever draws close to me by a cubit, I will draw close to him by a fathom. Whoever comes to me walking, I will come to him running."

Ilario's great lesson had become flesh and blood for him. Taking leave of him we cannot fail to remember the words that Roberto Assagioli said to Luisa Lunelli a few days after the death of his son: "His eyes see quite another Sun today!"

CONSOLIDATION OF THE WORK

After Ilario's death, life resumed its course, although we must keep in mind the words of Professor Leo Magnino from Rome, who knew Assagioli before the war and continued to visit him even after his move to Florence: "Assagioli had an enormous, I would say fascinating enthusiasm for all that life is, although unfortunately then there was the death of his son. Ilario's departure blocked his eagerness for life a little . . ."

However, the activities started again.

"In Florence Assagioli was highly esteemed," says Dr. Massimo Rosselli, former director of the Institute in Florence and a personal pupil of the master:

> Everyone in Florentine culture passed by here to listen to Assagioli's lessons at least once: analysts, psychiatrists, psychologists: they all came. He was esteemed, even though he was considered a somewhat unusual man, not easily classified. At that time, the inclusiveness of psychosynthesis, its marriage of East and West, was hardly understood. Now, things have changed: psychosynthesis is a psychology that can also be accepted by academics. Assagioli was a pioneer and paid the price for being one. But his psychosynthesis will be the psychology of the future, the psychology for the new era.

In addition to conferences, annual psychosynthesis courses, lessons, individual and group therapies (Assagioli was a pioneer of these), there were trips. Every year, until the 1970s (he died in 1974), Assagioli went to England, where he had meditation groups; to Paris, where there was an important psychosynthesis center that still exists; and to America, where his ideas had met with considerable interest.

THE YEARS OF MATURITY

The summer holidays were spent in Capolona, in the Arezzo countryside, and here Assagioli periodically organized conferences on the topics of psychosynthesis, Eastern religions and philosophies, and culture in general. There were conferences, or rather meetings for a few scholars, 10-15 people, among whom Assagioli managed to create a particular harmony. "The relationships were very human," said Professor Leo Magnino, who often participated:

> In Capolona there was an atmosphere that allowed everyone to put themselves on the same level as the Master — even if he didn't want to be called that. It was the same atmosphere that also existed at the Institute, but Capolona was in the open countryside and the influence of nature is very important for a person dedicated to spiritual research: Assagioli knew it well and was a great lover of nature!

As we have already mentioned, in Florence Assagioli received many people who came from all over the world to meet him. Periodically he had ordinary guests; also paying clients, and especially foreigners who spent periods with him to work and do their personal psychosynthesis. Assagioli had both serious patients, psychotic patients, and people who came for personal growth. This was perhaps the aspect that interested him most, because psychosynthesis is essentially a psychology for the healthy person; or rather, to use Sergio Bartoli's words, it is "the art of educating yourself." Assagioli acted as a discreet but attentive guide in this apprenticeship.

The actual students, the "continuers," those who have carried psychosynthesis forward, arrived relatively late, from the beginning of the sixties onwards: Sergio Bartoli, Bruno Caldironi, Piero Ferrucci, Massimo Rosselli, Alberto Alberti, Giorgio Fresia, Andrea Bocconi, and others we will meet in the next chapter. Assagioli dedicated a lot of time and attention to them, like a father, aware of the fact that there was no longer much time available, and that therefore it was necessary to train those to whom he would pass the torch.

"He was very welcoming to young people," says Massimo Rosselli, "always serene, joyful, always with a wonderful smile."

> He had infinite, radiant eyes that broke any rigidity. I came to him with problems and immediately these were put into perspective in a smiling and direct way. Not downplayed, but *downsized*. He was the embodiment of what he taught. His message and the spirituality of daily life: I met him as an old man, but I know he was like that even as a young man, despite the hard life he had . . .

Although very focused on his psychosynthesis, Roberto Assagioli was always aware of the facts of political and social life and, although not participating in public affairs, he did not neglect to express his thoughts. He did it in his indirect and discreet way, but also with great clarity, through a writing in which he refers to the Jewish tradition, while at the same time drawing inspiration from truly universal, ecumenical principles.

At the beginning of his essay entitled "What Would Isaiah Say Now?"[110] Assagioli wonders how an ancient prophet like Isaiah would solve "the religious, intellectual, moral and social problems of our times . . . with regard to which we are obliged to take a position?" The answers that Assagioli attributes to the prophet ("he would condemn . . . He would urge," etc.) actually express his own thought and therefore deserve to be succinctly reported for a better knowledge of Assagioli himself.

Assagioli begins with his disappointment with the religious field, noting that Isaiah, today as in the past, would condemn all forms of idolatry and fanatic nationalism, and instead would support true spiritual and human values, both individual and collective. In the social field Isaiah would be "a bold and courageous innovator," capable of fighting for a fair and just social order, for freedom and justice, and against any form of racism.

Isaiah, says Assagioli, "would never accept the Marxist doctrine, because his spiritual conception of life and his deep conviction of the divine direction of human history is incompatible with the principle of historical materialism." Eloquent words, which speak for themselves.

In the political field, the paper continues, Isaiah would have been guided by his religious principles, since the plan of God is to establish peace among the nations. "Therefore," says Assagioli, "he would be favorable towards the United Nations but he would constantly admonish its members to have more faith in its basic spiritual tenets and in those proclaimed in the Atlantic Charter; he would urge them to apply these principles more insistently and courageously." Isaiah would also work to eliminate the barriers that divide peoples and would "strongly" advise the richer nations to help the less favored ones.

Looking to the future, the prophet would point toward two alternatives: a new world war, which would have catastrophic consequences; or "the great vision of the new era," and of course he would work to ensure that the second hypothesis was realized. And this is all Assagioli, with his love for peace and concern for man's destinies.

---

[110] *Quotations from this essay are taken from a typed English-language manuscript that was found in the papers of the Psychosynthesis Research Foundation by this editor. —Ed.*

The last reflections concern the Jewish people themselves and reveal all of Assagioli's balance. Isaiah, he says, would invite Jews to renounce the exclusive attachment to their past, the accentuation of their particularism, excessive nationalism, and the importance given to material interests. And he would try to convince them that by virtue of their moral sense, their pure monotheism, their tradition, they have a *much higher and broader task*: that of promoting the spiritual regeneration of humanity. This task, continues Assagioli, would certainly attract the enthusiasm of young people, who by their nature are open to all that is great and generous. And in this too we find Assagioli himself, who throughout his life never tired of inviting mankind to look upwards and to work for growth and the common good.

Tolerance, moral sense, spirit of cooperation, love for peace, spirituality: these are the principles that Assagioli invites us to apply in the social and political field. Assagioli knew this well: today as then, these principles are the only ones capable of guaranteeing peace between peoples and individuals.

CHAPTER 3
ROBERTO ASSAGIOLI UP CLOSE

Roberto Assagioli was a man of our time. Relatively few years have passed since his death (1974) and as a result, I met numerous people who knew him: friends, relatives, acquaintances, colleagues, students, continuers of his work. Everyone has shown their willingness to share their experience with the father of psychosynthesis, and I am deeply grateful to everyone for their help and collaboration.[111]

I will start with the account of Ms. Luisa Lunelli, whom I have already had occasion to mention several times.

LUISA LUNELLI
"Life as a Journey"

As we have already seen, Ms. Lunelli (d.1993) had been a friend of the Assagioli family since the 1930s. She approached Assagioli for treatment, but she never became his patient; that first meeting marked the beginning of a friendship that was to last a lifetime. Luisa Lunelli is the author of a valuable essay entitled "Roberto, Nella and Luisa" published by the *Centro Studi R. Assagioli* of Florence, from which I have already quoted various passages. Other information that appears in the following interview is the result of a personal meeting in Bologna.

What was Roberto Assagioli like up close?

> He was simple. Simple and serene despite the difficulties of family and social life. He was serene even when his son died, whom he loved very much. Ilario's death devastated Nella. Roberto was on another level: having Ilario here or there was almost the same thing. He knew that man is more spirit

---

[111] *These interviews were conducted before the original publication in 1995. Since that time some of the interviewees have died. When possible the brief biographical data has been updated. —Ed.*

than matter, and spirit does not die. Ilario was ready too, he had accepted it. He was very religious, he was a Franciscan tertiary.[112]

What was Assagioli's position towards religion?

Roberto was not a practitioner, and he did not go to the synagogue despite having always remained formally Jewish. He had enormous admiration for the figure of Jesus and a great respect for all religions, even though he practiced none. He was at a level where it is no longer necessary to have a specific religion.

What relationship did Assagioli have with life, with daily affairs?

He traveled through life; he went through it, accepting it with a serene commitment: life as a journey . . . Psychosynthesis was his task: he knew he had something new to say in psychology, he had intuitions that he completed and enriched with his studies. This was his purpose in life, and he pursued it with extraordinary constancy and will.

What did it mean to you to know and associate with Assagioli?

It has been very important in my life to know him. He conveyed his serenity and above all his moral strength: he was modest, never raised his voice, never put himself forward, but had a great energy that he never flaunted. He achieved everything effortlessly, he reached the high and difficult goals he had set for himself by measuring out his strength with will. He taught me inner strength. He did not give direct lessons: he transformed [others] by living examples. By his way of being he gave a great deal to his family and to everyone around him — whoever was with him was transformed. He had very little of the air of a lecturer or professor; he did not advertise himself in any way. He had a humility that made him respectful toward others. I do not remember hearing any hostile phrases, negative judgments, or even simple dislike coming from his mouth. The word "defect" did not exist in his vocabulary: the defects were "different

---

[112] *A Franciscan tertiary, a member of the "third order of St. Francis," which was founded by St. Francis for secular people including married people who live a religious life but do not take vows or wear religious habit. —Ed.*

qualities," or qualities that were not cultivated or used improperly. He "healed" people who were near him without sessions, without medicines!

Would you share a particular memory of Assagioli?

The moments of meditation. To those who lived in his house, Roberto did not ask for any particular spiritual practice; he offered [something on] only two occasions. One was by opening the door of his study every day at noon. This was an invitation to enter for meditation. It was about twenty minutes of silent meditation, followed by the recitation of the Great Invocation aloud. The other opportunity offered was the celebration of the full moon. He observed it in the dining room around the big table. He read the statement he had himself prepared that, in addition to the description of the meanings and influences of the sign, which was new every year, also contained practical references to the present. Forty minutes or even an hour of silent meditation followed — [this was] "very good," as sometimes Roberto himself observed with satisfaction.

Then we left in silence. The group consisted of the family, some occasional guests, some close friends. On appropriate dates, the full moon was celebrated by Roberto for the general public in the meeting room on the ground floor of the building. Those moments of meditation I remember with particular intensity: I often had the opportunity to participate . . .

DONATELLA CIAPETTI ASSAGIOLI
"Nemo propheta patria" — "No man is a prophet in his own country."

Donatella (1934-2022) was the daughter of Nella's brother, who at the age of 21 — due to family problems — went to live with her aunt and uncle in 1955, [effectively] taking the place of Ilario, who had died four years earlier. Even before, she had lived with them frequently, especially in the summer in the countryside and during the war years. She had been very close to Ilario. Donatella stayed with her aunt and uncle for four years, then went to study in England. She married and returned with her husband to live in their home, on the top floor of the house in Via San Domenico. In those years she took an active part in the Meeting and Collaboration Center with Ms. Tina Muzzi, of whom we have already spoken. Together with Roberto and Nella, she helped establish the Psychosynthesis

Institute at its Florence location. Roberto Assagioli would have liked Donatella to continue his work, but she followed other paths, although today she works as a therapist. Donatella's marriage lasted seven years and ended in separation. She later lived in Rome, remarried and returned to Florence shortly before her uncle died. Because of her long association with Roberto Assagioli, Donatella Ciapetti is a valuable witness.

What struck you most about your uncle?

> Serenity, love, the ability to give without asking for anything in return. He gave a lot and didn't judge. He had his opinions about people, but he didn't judge. And he could be peaceful no matter what happened, even when they arrested him and put him in prison. Living with him has been very important to me from an evolutionary point of view: no one else has given me the encouragement that he has given me. Without words, without imposing his ideas, only by example. Jokingly he threw important seeds between one word and another. He never forced anything; he tactfully made things understood. He gave teachings appropriate to the age of the person, and he never made anyone uncomfortable because there was so much love in his words. He was very wise and profoundly good.

Is it true that he was involved in astrology?

> Yes, he was a real expert, and so was Ilario. In some cases, he also did his patients' horoscope. Personally he was of the sign of Pisces and therefore knew that he was not very strong-willed. Consequently, he worked hard to overcome this aspect: in his psychosynthesis the will is very important. My aunt, on the other hand, was Scorpio, alternating times of great enthusiasm and times of reserve. Theirs was an excellent marriage.

Were Judaism and esotericism important for Roberto Assagioli?

> His Jewish origin certainly was a weight or burden in his character, and it was something he always tried to overcome. For example, he ate everything, even pork, because he considered these prohibitions to be limits. Although he did not attend the synagogue, he was considered an important person in the Jewish community. And not only in Italy: once I was with him in Amsterdam and we

went together to the synagogue. I had to stop at the balustrade while he went over and was greeted with great deference by the rabbis, who accompanied him on the other side.[113] When he founded the Meeting and Collaboration Center here in Florence, the chief rabbi came and gave open support to the initiative.

As for esotericism, I can certainly say that my uncle was a true theosophist: his mother had been, and his wife had been introduced to theosophy by her mother, my grandmother Eloisa. Theosophy was very important for him, and he embraced it in its universal, non-religious sense, so there was no conflict even with his Jewish background. Psychosynthesis relies heavily on the breadth of view in theosophy and on the concept of evolution.[114] My uncle also believed in reincarnation, but he only talked about it in small groups. I remember him saying, "We are no longer thieves, murderers and prostitutes, because we have already been." Alice Bailey's teaching was also important; my uncle was in touch with her as long as she lived, and they met often. He knew Colonel Olcott, the friend and collaborator of Helena P. Blavatsky, with whom she had founded the Theosophical Society; they wrote, and met in London. My uncle also knew and contacted Annie Besant, the successor in Blavatsky's work. Esotericism was basic for him, but he kept his esoteric and scientific interests separate, because he didn't want to be misunderstood. However, certain practices, such as that of meditation, which he practiced habitually and openly, came from the East: he had adapted the visualizations to our Western mentality; for example, instead of the image of the lotus flower, he used that of the opening rose.

Did Assagioli travel a lot?

Yes, a lot. He went to America, England, Switzerland, and France, because the first psychosynthesis centers were founded there. More than once I heard him say with some bitterness *"Nemo propheta in patria."*[115] It was something that he suffered from a little. In 1957 I went with him to the United States and I realized how he was received: he was highly appreciated! His house was very popular, many foreigners came to study with him.

---

[113] *In traditional synagogues, men and women are seated separately. The women are in a balcony which often features a low balustrade that offers an open view of the rest of the sanctuary.* —Ed.

[114] *The theosophical and psychosynthetic meanings of "evolution," which involve a transpersonal and cosmic framework, are quite different from the Darwinian approach, which is purely materialistic.* —Ed.

[115] *A quotation from Luke 4:24 in Latin, which transliterates as "No prophet is accepted in his own country."* —Ed.

Is Assagioli understood as he deserves to be, today?

> In my opinion, no: He has not been well understood yet; he is not well known. But understanding is bound to grow, because psychosynthesis is the psychology of the future.

AMEDEO ROTONDI
"A great soul who returned here to teach."

Amedeo Rotondi (1908-1999) was a writer and owner of the well-known *Occasions Bookstore* (a.k.a. *The Rotondi Bookshop*) in Via Merulana in Rome, which specialized in psychological, esoteric and philosophical texts. He met Assagioli after the war and had a cordial relationship with him for many years.

When did you meet Assagioli?

> In 1949. He had already returned to Florence, but he often came to Rome to hold meetings in Ms. Batà's house, where there was talk of spiritual things. The first time I went, I heard the OM chanted, and it surprised me, because I am a Catholic. Later I understood and learned many things from him.

What impression did he have on you?

> I immediately felt that he was not an ordinary man. He was a very attractive, cultured, kind figure, who knew how to combine psychology with esotericism and spirituality. He came to me to get books, or to give me a list of people to send certain texts to at Christmas and Easter. Modest, avoiding controversy, he had quietly and discreetly separated himself from psychoanalysis. He had made synthesis, which is superior to analysis, his complete cosmic vision. Psychoanalysis is based on instincts. He wanted to go further, and in fact psychosynthesis teaches one how to put on wings. He was a hieratic figure, such as there are no longer. He wore a beard with the dignity with which the ancients wore it.

What did he teach you?

> To feel things, not to think superficially; to make the synthesis that incorporates strengths and weaknesses, 360 degrees [i.e., all around]. To see actions and intentions. He himself was the synthesis of what is most beautiful in all religions and philosophies. He was a great soul who came back here to teach . . .

SERGIO BERNARDI
"A Vertical Vision in a Horizontal World"

Professor Sergio Bernardi of Rome, professor of philosophy and great lover of psychology and Eastern disciplines, met Assagioli in 1947 for a personal problem, and received a lot of help. He later did a didactic analysis with him and visited him regularly for several years in Florence, where he had a university post.

What did you learn from Roberto Assagioli?

> That everything that happens takes place on the basis of what we think and feel, and that consequently many external phenomena depend on our interiority. So the way we live is important, our interiority. Assagioli made me understand that the conscious makes plans, but the unconscious runs on programs without conscious knowledge. He was a superior person, very generous, who really tried to help others and knew how to give initiatory pushes. Like all initiates, he led others to identify with him and to follow him on his way. There was a special atmosphere around him, as is always the case with initiates. He was very valuable as a man: he knew how to make a deep impact, how to set archetypes in motion, to provoke . . .

You have a profound knowledge of psychoanalysis and knew C. G. Jung well. How did Assagioli stand with relation to Freud and Jung?

> Assagioli was the first to speak of Freud in Italy, with articles in the magazine *Psiche*.[116] He accepted the method of investigation, but not other aspects,

---

[116] As well as articles in Rivista di psicologia applicata alla Pedagogia e alla Psicopatologia and La Voce and other periodicals. —Ed.

such as the Oedipus complex, the *Superego*, and the *id*. His vision of the psyche was different from Freud's: at the top he saw the Self, the spirit, what Jung called *Selbst* and the Indians call *Atman*. Freud was a pioneer, but he had removed spirituality, in my opinion; so Jung's break from him was inevitable. Jung was closer to Assagioli, but did not share his enthusiasm for Alice Bailey; he also did not agree with Rudolf Steiner, who believed that everyone could achieve initiation. He thought that only the mature can be awakened. Jung was possessed by energies he had learned to master: he talks about it in his *Memories*. He felt that there are problems that go beyond those of ordinary men. Freud could not be his teacher in this. With Assagioli, on the other hand, there was understanding precisely on these points, on the spiritual vision and esoteric interests. Assagioli cared a lot about spirituality: his was a vertical vision in a horizontal world which doesn't want to know . . .

SERGIO BARTOLI
"An Ancient Soul"

Dr. Sergio Bartoli (1929-2009), a physician and psychotherapist from Rome was one of the people who was closest to Assagioli in the last years of his life. In this interview he himself tells how they met and what developed from their meeting. Dr. Bartoli was director of the Psychosynthesis Center in Rome for many years, and co-founder of The Italian Society of Psychosynthesis Therapy (SIPT). He lived most of the year in Città della Pievè,[117] where he created *Poggio del Fuoco*, (now called *Comunità di Etica Vivente*, [*Community of Ethical Living*]), a center that offers programs that use aspects of psychosynthesis, especially meditation. His account is particularly important because it allowed him to frame Roberto Assagioli both as a person, as a scholar, and as a "Master."

How did you meet Roberto Assagioli?

Almost by chance in 1964. I was an internist in Rome and as a hobby I was involved in psychology and psychoanalysis. Some friends one day gave me handouts by Assagioli, whom I didn't know. What I read struck me with clarity and simplicity; they were things that were familiar to me, things that

---
[117] *Just west of the city of Perugia in Tuscany. —Ed.*

I also thought, so I decided to go and see him. When I knocked on his door, it was opened by a maid surrounded by dogs and cats who jumped on everyone, which was unusual for me. I saw other female figures coming and going; the house had quaint little things that revealed a fascination with details and also a certain Eastern-style mysticism. Then I entered Assagioli's study. He was 76 years old and did not wear it well. He had become rather stooped, with a white beard, thick glasses, and a chamber jacket. I was expecting a completely different person, a professor . . . I was confused. He asked me the reason for my visit and I told him about the handouts that I had read that had struck me with their clarity. He was glad that a colleague was interested in his work. It was a fairly generic meeting, concerning knowledge; however, I was a little uncomfortable because he was not the person I had expected. I went out thinking that we would never see each other again. He had the secretary give me some material and we said goodbye. That first contact left no trace in me: I was expecting a doctor, and instead I had found a guru. This had been my first impression, even though he was very wise and nothing he said was out of balance. It was his physical image in particular that struck me in this sense. Months went by and an Argentine doctor telephoned me. He had been a patient of Assagioli's and had become passionate about psychosynthesis; he wanted to lecture in Rome to make it known, and on behalf of Assagioli he asked me to help him. He also told me that Assagioli had invited me to organize a congress of psychosynthesis in Rome. I was a little surprised by this request, but I found a conference room for the Argentine doctor and gave him some help in the organization. I went back to Assagioli with him and we got to know each other better. Then in 1967 there was the international congress of psychosomatic medicine in Rome[118] organized by Professor Ferruccio Antonelli, a psychosomatic doctor, who is still president of the Society of Psychosomatic Medicine, and a large portion of the conference was dedicated to psychosynthesis. Roberto Assagioli presented the plenary talk, and many people came to listen to him. It was a success for him and for psychosynthesis. In the meantime my relationship with him had deepened and I was starting to get into the spirit of psychosynthesis. His physical frailty, his wisdom, his inspired air (he was an inspired man!) were winning me over.

---

[118] In connection with this, see the subsequent interview with Professor Ferruccio Antonelli.

What was your relationship to him?

He was the good father to me: I had a difficult relationship with my father's authority, and this man was always so smiling, so accepting! I was 42 years old at the time, and he immediately told me to speak to him as an equal, since we were colleagues. I did not do this for the first two years, because I saw him as an authority.

When did you really start collaborating?

When he asked me to open a center in Rome. He had created one in 1926, then he had to close it before the war because he was persecuted as a Jew. At that time I had no interest in doing such a thing. I was a well-established doctor, I had a family and professional life structured in a certain way. But I ended up opening the center: I found a location, a kind of basement in Via Monte Zebio, made available by a friend, and I began to spread psychosynthesis in Rome.[119]

In the evening I held my little chats: I brought Assagioli's handouts, I read and talked with the people who came: psychologists, spiritualists, some young people, many elderly people, some Masons — in short, what is found in Rome whenever there are initiatives of this kind. One must keep in mind there was a collision of this approach with my own basically materialistic training, even though my father had been a lover of esotericism and I had read books on yoga, magic, etc. as a boy. So I had my own general knowledge on the subject [of esotericism]. Assagioli was very careful to keep his psychosynthesis separate from esotericism, but it was known that he dealt with it, and consequently many people who had the same interests came. At some point I rebelled against this situation, and there was a certain tension at the Roman center; however Assagioli always supported me by saying that I was the director and that I should do as I thought best.

---

[119] Later the center of Rome changed its location. Dr. Bartoli directed it for many years. The subsequent director was Ms. Girelli Macchia, great connoisseur of Assagioli's work, translator of *The Act of Will* and curator of the volume *Transpersonal Development*, both by Roberto Assagioli. *The current director is Elena Merghi.—Ed.*

Assagioli must have liked you, as well as esteem you very much.

I think so. For my part, over time, without realizing it, I became very protective of Assagioli, who was not always well understood by the official psychology and psychoanalysis: his books were evaluated in a slightly "caustic" way. He was accused of wanting to reintroduce the concept of soul by bringing it back through the window after it had been put out by the door. I defended him, with reactions that were even rather harsh towards these colleagues. Assagioli scolded me for this and one day he put one of his famous notes in my pocket with the words: *Correct your impulsiveness.* He made me correct, even if not entirely, what he believed to be the three major defects of my character: impulsiveness, hypercriticism and a certain degree of "scatteredness." He said that I was doing too many things: I calmed down . . . Meanwhile, I had taken psychosynthesis very much to heart and I had opened myself to psychiatric and psychological discourse as my possible medical practice: I had been an internist, then I had become a psychosomatic doctor with Antonelli, and now I was becoming a psychotherapist. Assagioli pushed me a lot in this sense, encouraging me, and reassuring me, as I did not feel I had the credentials from a psychological point of view. Those were the heroic times of psychotherapy: I did my personal analysis and I really started to find myself.

Psychosynthesis had therefore conquered you . . .

The more time passed, the more he convinced me. The relationship with Assagioli was extremely fascinating. I felt safe, actually. Little by little I learned. Whatever question I asked he answered, after a moment of silence — but the things he said were shocking in my opinion, because they were so broad that I didn't grasp them immediately. He had the ability to interpret anything with a vast vision and consciousness. He became a model for me, not in the sense of personal identification because I was too different from him, but in the sense of asking myself what he would have done in that situation . . .

Someone said that meeting with Assagioli was like getting a big hug. Do you agree?

Yes. He was a "love" type. His wisdom helped me a lot. I always went to him and I always felt very welcomed, even though he certainly saw all my limitations, my impetuosity and impulsiveness, and the scientific-mindedness that was obsessive for me at that time. For me, what was unscientific was to be left out — a little like Piero Angela.[120] If I think about it now, I get goosebumps!

Assagioli is often compared to C.G. Jung: is this a correct comparison in your opinion?

I didn't know Jung personally, but I did an analysis with a psychiatrist from Milan who had been a direct student of Jung and who also knew Assagioli well, with whom she had also been a collaborator for a time. I asked her what the differences were between Assagioli and Jung and she replied, "Jung was an intelligent, charming, very nice man. Assagioli is a *guru*." I discovered that it was true: Assagioli's dominant note was a different state of consciousness. He was an enlightened one, although it may be difficult for some people to accept this description. Certainly he was an extraordinary person — anyone who had contact with him realized it. At first I lived with this situation with some embarrassment, but then I understood — after his death — that he had experienced this state of [higher] consciousness and that this was his message; therefore psychosynthesis had to be a model in which each of us could grow our consciousness. On the similarities and differences between Jung's psychosynthesis and psychology, Assagioli himself wrote many things: just read his handouts.[121]

What is psychosynthesis for you?

It is not a model that can be taught like psychoanalysis; psychosynthesis goes beyond psychoanalysis: it was conceived as the psychology of the healthy man, while psychoanalysis was conceived as the psychology of the sick man. Psychosynthesis was not conceived as therapy, it is a philosophy of life — a psychology for the man who wants to grow, a practice to harmonize all psychic functions, reintegrating the unconscious, creating a center of harmony so that it becomes the Self: the soul expressed, witnessed, lived, manifested. Jung approached the soul as an act of faith; Assagioli experienced it: he was in contact with his Self.

---

[120] Piero Angela was a science journalist and the host of a long-running science show in Italy.

[121] *One of those handouts was an article titled "Jung and Psychosynthesis," published by the Psychosynthesis Research Foundation as PRF Issue No. 19 in 1967, and now available online at* https://kennethsorensen.dk/en/c-g-jung-and-psychosynthesis/. *—Ed.*

I think of those answers [from him] that seemed to come from above, from another dimension! Assagioli was very gifted by nature; he had been very precocious, and he had a rare lucidity and clarity. His was an inner, spiritual super-gift. He was a great soul, let's say an *ancient soul*, who had gained a certain experience in his history. He believed in reincarnation, although he did not speak openly about it, perhaps because he had some obtuse co-workers — with me at the front of the line. I remember he suggested that I read Alice Bailey's esoteric psychology. I read those books, found them absurd, and abandoned them. He, with great common sense, did not comment. After a few years I picked up those books again, found them interesting and told him so. He looked me straight in the eye and said, "I'm glad for you." A different vision of life was emerging in me.

You stayed with Assagioli until his death, didn't you?

Yes. But when he died, I was on a boat with friends and they could not reach me. When I returned to Rome I was informed: I ran to Florence, but he had already been cremated. It produced a strong emotion for me, the first I had experienced as an adult. I, who was not easily moved, felt lost at not finding him in his little study anymore. I slept for a few nights in his house, and the night after my arrival I had a dream. I say it was a dream, although I am sure it was something more. It was a contact. I still remember the liveliness of that meeting: I had never dreamed of Assagioli before and I never dreamed of him after. I said to him: "Roberto! — but then you're not dead, thank goodness that we have met. I didn't know you were sick, I was on the boat . . ." He looked at me very seriously, which he never did, and said to me: "Ah, you came!" And I said, "Yes, but if you have really died, what do we do with the institute? You didn't say who is to succeed you, what are we going to do?" After all, it was a considerable cultural and real estate enterprise to manage and I felt lost. He looked at me very seriously and said, "This is now your problem, yours in particular. I am no longer involved, I have other things to do." He said it with great detachment. I was very disappointed by that meeting, but since that day I have taken a responsibility for psychosynthesis on my shoulders. I did it with my own character, and therefore sometimes in an abrupt and combative way. However, I continued to come regularly to Florence and to have my point of reference at the Institute, which was gradually becoming a clinic. I joined the Board of Directors in Florence and supported Ida Palombi, who became president of the Institute. When a master dies, there are always difficulties. Assagioli *was* the Institute, and collecting his legacy was not easy. In fact, initially there were divisions among us; but now there is more harmony, even if each of us has chosen his own line of research. Assagioli proposed many different stimuli and psychosynthesis is not a dogmatic principle, it is a vision of life applicable to many fields.

You spoke a lot about Assagioli's qualities: did you also find flaws in him?

In my opinion he had an excess of loving kindness that led him to become attached to people or situations. He was very sensitive, and this excessive sensitivity unnerved him a little — it made him sometimes less productive than he could have been. Maybe his age was a factor — he had been more combative when he was young. His receptivity, his availability were excessive: he saw quality in everyone and found that I was too rigid in my assessments. Assagioli's personality did not fascinate me: I was fascinated by his soul and his work.

What was Roberto Assagioli for you?

At different times in my life, a different character. First the good father, a figure with whom I had affectionate experience. I didn't do the analysis with him, but he did give me supportive psychotherapy and didactic supervision. He also gave me advice. Then there was the collaborative relationship when I opened the Center under his supervision. When he died, I discovered a different energy, a different consciousness — a spiritual guide? Maybe yes. I tried to bring psychosynthesis into my life as he had done until his death: to the end he used the evocative words, which are a technique of psychosynthesis. When I asked him why, he replied that there is never an end to our personal psychosynthesis. In the last period of his life he was deaf: you had to write questions to him. When he noticed the uneasiness of a speaker, he said, "It is an advantage to become deaf, because I only hear what suits me." In Assagioli I found different points of reference according to the maturity of my consciousness. For me, Assagioli was a great man who left a message to those who are able to grasp it. As I have already mentioned, there has been a split in the identity of psychosynthesis, and each of us disciples has grasped one aspect of it, what was most congenial to him: the therapeutic, the social or the transpersonal aspect. I opted for meditation and the transpersonal, because today this is what I feel is fundamental for me and for others.

How would you define psychosynthesis?

As the psychology of the future. Assagioli hypothesized a broader and more defined personality structure than what Jung envisaged — he glimpsed an infinite projection of consciousness. Psychosynthesis has recovered ancient traditions by combining and integrating Eastern and Western culture, and it has brought together the most significant aspects of these two worlds by marrying their antithetical aspects. Psychosynthesis is an admirable synthesis of everything that man has intuited. It is as simple as a great synthesis can be; the method is easy to handle, within everyone's reach and usable. It helps those who are troubled on a personal level and also gives an answer to those who seek contact with their soul, with their Self.

What aspects seem most original to you in psychosynthesis?

There are many. Its ability to improve inter-individual relationships seems important to me, because it shows ways to integrate different people with common goals. This is an aspect that Assagioli personally took me to task for: he had the ability to perceive potential that had been ignored. At that time I felt very individualistic and preferred the relationship between doctor and patient, and I ignored group work. So he invited me to write something about social psychosynthesis, about groups. I was amazed; I never expected such a thing. I thought he didn't understand me, but I started to deal with it. This was in 1965-66, and very little was being done with groups at the time. But over time group psychotherapy and dynamics has become my preferred path. I quit individual psychotherapy and am involved with the formation of groups. I believe that the group is the structure of the future, and I believe that our consciousness must become group consciousness.

Assagioli had great faith in man, didn't he?

Yes, he saw the healthy aspects in man, projected into the future. Psychosynthesis is characterized not so much by man's attention to the past, which is a metabolism that has already occurred, but by the identification of healthy, future aspects. Psychosynthesis has taught me to say: I live to build the future, mine and that of the world. Every day that passes is like putting a wall behind me, and from there I have to go on. Psychoanalysis looks to the past and the deep bottom, whereas psychosynthesis looks to the future and the profound heights.

Assagioli was therefore also a pioneer.

He was very much ahead of his time, and this has been one of his problems, especially in a country like Italy, which is very conservative culturally. Assagioli's proposal was too detached from traditional culture. Gradually, however, understanding grows. Assagioli's psychosynthesis is ultimately the art of educating oneself, and he did it continuously. All of life is a permanent process of self-education, and psychosynthesis provides the tools. These are new, innovative concepts, and for this reason Assagioli was a pioneer. There are still many things to discover in him!

FERRUCCIO ANTONELLI
"An Infinite Respect for the Patient"

Professor Ferruccio Antonelli (1927-2000) was a professor of psychiatry at the University of Rome and Catholic University of the Sacred Heart in Milan, a specialist in nervous and mental illnesses and President of the Italian Society of Psychosomatic Medicine, and founder of the Italian Association of Sports Psychology.

Professor, how did you meet Roberto Assagioli?

I met Roberto Assagioli personally in his Florentine study in Via San Domenico in 1966, but we had already known each other by name for several years, and we had exchanged some publications to keep us up to date with each other's studies. In those days there were so few of us who dealt with psychosomatics that it was natural to get to know each other and be friends.

I went to see him because I was organizing the Seventh European Biennial Conference on Psychosomatic Research, a task that had been assigned to me in Athens the year before. I wanted to live up to the prestigious task and not disappoint the European colleagues who wanted to meet in Rome after the previous congresses in London, Amsterdam, Copenhagen, Hamburg, Madrid, and Athens. Furthermore, for us Italian psychosomatologists, it was an important as well as delicate opportunity to get out of the "semi-clandestinity" into which we had been forced by an academic world that was very cautious if not downright skeptical towards psychosomatics. In my opinion, the 1967 congress was to be a "historic" event, and indeed it was. It was actually the first world congress on psychosomatics in history. It was supposed to be the "presentation to the temple" — the temple of contemporary culture — of the Italian psychosomatic movement, supported by a credible international sponsorship.

Thus the European congress was included in a larger structure, called "International Psychosomatic Week," which included the "VII European Conference on Psychosomatic Research," the "First National Congress of the Italian Society of Psychosomatic Medicine" (SIMP), the "First National Congress of the Italian Society for the Study of Hypnosis"(AMISI), an "International Conference on Psychosomatic Cancer," an "International Symposium on Research into the Psychophysiology of Sleep," the "First Symposium of the Italian Society of Obstetric Psychoprophylaxis," an International Symposium of Military Psychosomatics, an International Symposium on Pharmacological Problems in Psychosomatics, an International Symposium of Psychosomatic Sports Medicine, and the "Fifth International Conference on Psychosynthesis."

The latter event was conducted with Assagioli who was immediately and happily available to offer his maximum collaboration.

Was the congress successful?

It was a six-day congress, comprising ten different conferences or symposia, with central plenary sessions of masterful readings. A thousand participants from 43 countries produced 270 reports: five volumes of proceedings for a total of 1700 pages.

Assagioli presented his *main lecture* in the plenary session together with Michael Balint (creator of the Balint training groups[122]), Carlo L. Cazzullo

---

[122] *A Balint group is a purposeful, regular meeting among family physicians, with a trained facilitator or leader, to allow*

(the first psychiatrist at Palazzo Italia [in Milan] to "open" to psychosomatics),[123] Léon Chertok (the French pioneer of obstetric psychoprophylaxis, initially defined as "preparation for painless childbirth"),[124] Arthur Jores (medical doctor from Hamburg and founder of German psychosomatics),[125] Denis Leigh (president of the European Group for Psychosomatic Research and of the first European Conference, London 1954),[126] and Juan Rof Carballo (the highest authority on psychosomatics in Spanish psychiatry).[127] With these "magnificent seven," the session of 13 September 1967, in simultaneous translation, was the *highlight* of the entire International Psychosomatic Week. Assagioli's masterful reading was particularly appreciated. Its title was "Psychosomatic Medicine and Biopsychosynthesis." [128]

Can you try to summarize it?

Psychosynthesis (the *bio* prefix can be removed for convenience, but remains essential in the concept) has been grafted onto the trunk of psychoanalysis and is a psychotherapy that has two purposes: 1) *to eliminate conflicts,* [both] conscious and unconscious, which hinder complete and harmonious development of the personality, and 2) to *use active techniques* to stimulate the psychological functions that remain weak or immature.

The *bios* is obviously there, but psychosynthesis doesn't take specific interest in it. It "takes note" of it but thinks of other things. You don't need to know what electricity is to use it, says Assagioli, but we try to make the best use of it. The best outcome is to meet the needs and aspirations of the *higher unconscious* to achieve the two aforementioned objectives. This concept is original with psychosynthesis but was also intuited by other thinkers. Assagioli quotes Jores: many ailments derive from the frustration

---

discussion of any topic that occupies a physician's mind outside of his or her usual clinical encounters. —Ed.

[123] *Carlo L. Cazzullo (1915-2000) was the first Professor of Psychiatry at the University of Milan.* —Ed.

[124] Cf. Léon Chertok, *L'ipnosi. Teoria, pratica, tecnica,* [*Hypnosis: Theory, Practice, Technique*], Edizioni Mediterranee, Rome, 1992.

[125] *Arthur Jores (1901-1982) was a German physician and professor at the University of Hamburg.* —Ed.

[126] *Dr. A. Denis Leigh (1915-1998) was a British psychiatrist, one-time Secretary-General of the World Psychiatric Association.* —Ed.

[127] *Juan Rof Carballo (1905-1994) was a Spanish doctor, professor at the Central University of Madrid, who gave courses in psychosomatic medicine in Spain and many countries in South America.* —Ed.

[128] *This address was published as a pamphlet by the Psychosynthesis Research Foundation as PRF Issue No. 21 in 1967.* —Ed.

of an intimate need for *productivity* and personality *development*. He quotes Frankl: the *search for meaning* is a primary force of man; the values that give meaning to life do not *drive* a man but rather *attract* him. And he quotes Maslow: the highest intrinsic values, the spiritual life, the highest aspirations are *part* of human nature.

What values did Assagioli particularly appreciate?

In the hierarchy of values, Assagioli emphasizes the priority of the *will* with its various *stages* (goal, evaluation, purpose, deliberation, decision, planning, execution) and its various *qualities* (energy charge, inhibiting power, promptness, tenacity). And he appreciatively quotes Ancona:[129] motivation is identified with the will because when a man desires, he intends to do something, which is very different from being forced or solicited or eager; it is a behavior of anticipation in which reality is desired in the abstract before being implemented in practice. Even Jores thinks so: the will is the compass of human action: it is in this way that man has become a moral being.

The use of the will is very important for psychosomatic medicine. Assagioli believes that the *will to heal* is fundamental, that is, the "willing and active collaboration of the patient" — this is what is now called *compliance*.

What therapeutic techniques does psychosynthesis use?

To use Assagioli's words: "Coming to the specific field of therapy, psychosynthesis naturally takes a . . . synthetic position." That is, it makes use of all treatment techniques, suitably combining or alternating them. These techniques also include an examination of the [patient's] existential situation and personal conception of life and the world, given the importance of the higher unconscious. It is not philosophy, but even if it were, it is known that every human being has his own "philosophy," sometimes without even knowing it. Any mistake in facing the world and life can arouse emotions capable of somatization.[130] However, Assagioli specifies that psychosynthesis does not take metaphysical or religious positions, because it "reaches the threshold of the mystery and stops there." Therefore it is suitable for all

---

[129] *Leonardo Ancona (1922-2008) was an Italian psychologist and author.* —Ed.

[130] *Somatize: to express psychological issues through bodily or somatic symptoms.* —Ed.

patients "whatever their beliefs are."

In treating psychosomatic patients, psychosynthesis gives the appropriate weight to the "re-dimensioning" of the bodily experience. Some (materialists) give exaggerated importance to the body, others (intellectuals) give it too little. Therefore psychosynthesis can be used in combination with drugs, relaxation techniques, and physical activity.

What struck you most in the Assagioli lecture?

The last part of the master's presentation deals with the doctor-patient relationship, which is defined as follows: "A relationship that develops as the treatment proceeds and that creates a psychological interaction at various levels and of different types."

Personally I see in these words Assagioli's most authentic message — his style of interpreting the [role of the] psychotherapist, his infinite respect for the patient, his willingness to always be helpful: with charisma, humanity, suggestion, culture, empathy, rationality. However, he said, "various levels and different types:" words that make you think. The psychotherapist is called to operate in the existential dimension of the individual patient whatever their intellectual and cultural qualities, ethnic and family influences, frustrating or rewarding experiences, personal relationship with love, society, sexuality, work, spiritual life, art, or free time.

Psychotherapy is a work that cannot be practiced as "a profession;" it requires commitment, seriousness, training, both to help others and to avoid involvement. This is Assagioli's "lesson:" To follow.

Assagioli was one of a few great men who received widespread recognition in the world of science while he was still alive. The Fifth International Psychosynthesis Conference was also held at the Congress in Rome. His psychosynthesis had been established for many years in many countries. In Rome we listened to the reports of the Argentines Aleandri, Corazzi, Molteni; the French Bicart, Quertant, Nouvion, and De Chevron-Villette; the Canadians Taylor and Crampton; the Americans Gerard and Petitclerc; the Spaniard Ferrer Hombravella; the Swiss Faillettaz; and the Indian Agravai. There was nothing apologetic, but a chorus of consensus and confirmation in favor of a man and a technique — both of which are worthy of a prominent place in the history of medicine, psychology, and psychosomatics.

TERESA D'AMICO
"He is the most complete human being I have met."

Teresa D'Amico (1938-) studied with Roberto Assagioli for about ten years, after meeting him through Dr. Sergio Bartoli. Her relationship with the father of psychosynthesis was always very affectionate and filial. Teresa D'Amico currently lives between Rome and Umbria, where she teaches psychosynthesis courses for children and young people aged 8 to 18.

Signora, what struck you most in Roberto Assagioli?

> His demonstrating by example. Psychosynthesis is daily training, it is the responsibility for every moment. And he taught by giving a personal example: he was the living testimony for psychosynthesis. This is the legacy for all of us, his testament. He never used words unless they were deeply lived. I was also struck by his ability to love, which was enormous. He said: never hurt, never hurt, because evil comes back. I have never heard a criticism of anyone from him; he always invited us to be tolerant. He was very humble, he said that he had not yet learned to live, that one never stops learning to live, and in these words there is all of psychosynthesis, which is more training than therapy.

Is there anything you learned from him that continues to matter for your daily life?

> The exercise of disidentification, which has Eastern origins and which Assagioli adapted to the Western mentality. It teaches one not to identify with the body, with the role we play in life, with one's personality, and consequently to detach ourselves from the physical part in order to identify with the Self. If you do this every morning, it provides a suggestion that helps you detach yourself from fixed emotions and thoughts. It gives you the opportunity to understand who you are and where you are going. Assagioli taught people to walk in life: he said that you can fall, but that you must also get up. His eyes were always smiling, they trusted, they accepted you totally. He was the most complete human being I have ever met. After being with him for a day, I lived on that for months! When he died, I felt alone, but he had always told me that his [physical] presence was unnecessary and that he would help me even from afar. In fact he did help me, and I continue to feel his presence.

Who was Roberto Assagioli for you?

> The true man of the Age of Aquarius, a complete synthesis of mind and heart. His was a loving will, a will of the soul, that led him to acting consistently in life. He had a great energy beneath his sweet appearance. He was a beacon that had light for everyone. He was aware of it, but did not show it. He was also aware of having a task in life, but he was detached, he had no ambition. He went on day after day, step by step, and gave only what could be absorbed [by someone]. He was profoundly and totally authentic. And everyone felt it . . .

PIERO FERRUCCI
"A Great Spiritual Master"

Dr. Piero Ferrucci (1946 -) was a personal student of Roberto Assagioli and lived near him from 1969 to 1974. A graduate in philosophy, he is a psychotherapist and author of important books such as *What We May Be, Inevitable Grace* and *Introduction to Psychosynthesis*. After Assagioli's death, between 1974 and 1976, he organized the vast amount of material, mostly manuscripts, which had been left behind. In Florence he created the Centro Studi di Psicosintesi "R. Assagioli," and regularly collaborates with the Italian Society of Therapeutic Psychosynthesis (SIPT).

How did you meet Roberto Assagioli?

> I had been to the United States to study the techniques of humanistic psychology and at Esalen Institute I heard about Assagioli in such terms that I wanted to meet him. I wrote to him and went to find him. We met each other and Assagioli invited me to study with him. I was close to graduation: I moved to Florence and stayed close to him for five years, until his death. It was an extraordinary experience, one of the most beautiful in my life, for various reasons. Assagioli was the catalyst for my growth, and in a few years I matured much more than if I hadn't met him. He was a person with an enormous "charge" of joy, which he transmitted in an extraordinarily intense way to me and everyone: people who were sad, depressed, or "gray" came to him and after an hour they came out transformed, full of light and enthusiasm. This also had an effect on me. The most important thing, however, was that he activated a potential that I didn't even know I had.

For example?

It was he who suggested that I write, and this has been a seminal experience in my life. He said that writing is a form of service, a kind of magic in the sense that a book can bring light to many people; even if it is not a best seller, it can be a stimulus even after many years, it can act as a real spiritual message. He said that through books we are in contact with all the great spirits of humanity and he repeated that I, in my own small way, had to do this work — and I did it. Then it was Assagioli who helped me to become a psychotherapist, who offered me this professional possibility thanks to his basic assistance; and above all he opened the ways of the spirit to me and gave me a deeper sense of love, of joy, of will. I believe this is the greatest gift that can be done for a person. I then continued on this path.

In your opinion, what was Assagioli's most important influence?

Like the great spiritual Masters, he did not want to create groups or suggest belonging to this or that church, but he stimulated the highest and wisest part of us: he made us independent. I had a great desire for freedom, I didn't want to belong to a school and I told him that, by adhering to psychosynthesis, I didn't want to give up access to the great traditions and scientific currents that interested me. He agreed: he was a person who deeply respected the freedom of others. After his death a strange synchronistic event occurred, or perhaps it was a message from him: I met a person whom Assagioli, in their only meeting, had advised to read Emerson's essay "Self-Reliance," which is about confidence in oneself, autonomy over one's own person. In this work Emerson explains how important it is to base one's life not on the example of others, but on what we discover about ourselves: we must trust this. When that person told me these things, I received a great impression, it was as if Assagioli himself had said to me: Okay, now go ahead on your own . . .

Do you consider yourself a disciple of Assagioli?

Certainly. I learned a lot from him, I agree with the totality of what he said, and I feel a deep sense of gratitude for him. I was with him from ages 23 to 28, the formative years. Looking back on that time and revisiting it with more professional and life experience, I realized that he had a paternal role towards me; there was also a little transference, however my admiration for Assagioli is unchanged.

Who was Roberto Assagioli?

A highly evolved person spiritually; a true sage who was in contact with levels of consciousness not available to most people. He did not want to be a *guru* or a Master with a capital M, but an educator, a psychologist. However, he *was* a Master — I don't know if this was because he was "an ancient soul" or because he had become one. He knew how to touch people's souls; contact with him transformed one, psychologically and spiritually. This, along with joy and a *sense of humor*, was his main feature.

In the Italian cultural panorama, in what consideration is he held?

He is a figure that has been rigorously repressed by our whole culture: I realized this when I organized the conference for the centenary of his birth in 1988. There were speakers from 24 countries around the world, but only one local newspaper published a short article. When he died, nobody talked about it in Italy. He has been repressed and ignored, although his contribution was and is vital.

Why?

Our Italian culture works in terms of categories: Catholicism, communism, existentialism, and so on. If one is a "free hitter," if one is not involved in the parties, leagues or associations, it is difficult for one to be accepted. Then there is another aspect: Assagioli speaks of the transpersonal, and the repression of the sublime is a reality. These are things that embarrass many, for some they are even scary. He may be rediscovered, or others will use his ideas without mentioning him, as is already happening in certain American groups.

If he were alive, what would he say about this?

He would accept it with a smile, he would joke about it. The important thing for him was that the ideas are passed along.

Do you remember any particular episodes in Assagioli's life?

Yes, I can tell you a couple that seem very significant to me. The first concerns Lama Govinda, the German sage who lived for a long time in India and Tibet, a great expert on Tibetan mysticism. He came to Italy and went to visit Assagioli, who was on vacation in Castiglioncello. I was with him that day. It was a very nice meeting between two old men full of experience and wisdom, both with white beards, similar in some respects. While Lama Govinda went up the stairs, Assagioli asked me how he should greet him: in the Western manner with a handshake, or in the Eastern way with his hands folded and a bow. I suggested the Eastern greeting. Instead, Govinda held out his hand and Assagioli bowed, and there was a rather curious exchange. Then we left them alone to talk, and someone turned on a tape recorder; later I heard part of the dialogue. They were elderly, they could hardly hear each other, and each went on a little on their own, but it was not a dialogue between deaf people: there was a communion of souls, they were happy to have met. The meeting was at a different level than that of a mere intellectual conversation.

And the other episode?

It's about Nella, his wife, whom he loved very much. He had great patience with her, a great care for her, as she had become a little difficult in recent years. He too was old, and tired easily. One day he was working with me on his book on the will. She came in and asked him to go with her to receive her friends, because the ladies wanted to meet him. He had to choose between a commitment he cared about and something trivial. He chose to join his wife's friends; he gave priority to kindness.

Assagioli's last years are particularly rich in events, publications, and meetings. Isn't that strange in an 80-year-old man?

There is an episode that would explain it: it happened before I met him, when he was 77 or 78 years old. Ida Palombi, his secretary, told me about it, and Assagioli also told me something. He had to have prostate surgery, which was serious because he was in frail health. In the half-sleep after the operation, he said aloud, "No, no!" And then, after a while, "Okay, I'll do it!" He actually wanted to leave, because death for him was a birth into more joyful levels; however, there were still tasks to be done. Later he said to me, "They kicked me back!" In fact there was a flowering in the last few years: the new students, those of my generation; important acknowledgments, and the book on the will. It was then that Assagioli laid the foundations for the future work of psychosynthesis. If he died before then, perhaps psychosynthesis would have died out . . .

BRUNO CALDIRONI
"Psychosynthesis puts helium in the hot air balloon . . . "

Prof. Bruno Caldironi (1929-2015) was a neuropsychiatrist and psychotherapist from Ravenna, studied with Assagioli for the last seven years of his life. He was one of his most valuable and assiduous students and collaborators. He carried on the discourse of therapeutic psychosynthesis, with great energy and skill, and was president of the SIPT (Italian Society of Therapeutic Psychosynthesis) for many years. He was the author of various publications, including *Seminari di psicopatologia e psicoterapia* [*Seminars on Psychopathology and Psychotherapy*] (1992) and *L'umom a tre dimensioni: colloqui con Roberto Assagioli 1967-1971* [*Three Dimensional Man: Conversations with Roberto Assagioli 1967-1971*] (2005).

How and when did you meet Roberto Assagioli?

I met him in 1967 at the Congress of Psychosomatic Medicine organized in Rome by Professor Antonelli. I went because I had already heard about Assagioli years before. Since the 1950s I had been attending the Institute of Psychotherapy in Vienna, which at the time was directed by Viktor Frankl, and it was he who pointed me toward Assagioli, saying that I should meet him. The opportunity presented itself with the psychosomatic congress. I spent much time with Assagioli until his death: I was at his bedside when he died. In that same year — 1967 that is — I started studying with him, and that went on until 1971: two hours a week alone and an hour together with a colleague, Ferioli. Later we became collaborators.

What in particular did you deal with?

A little bit of all aspects of psychosynthesis. Assagioli also cared a lot about the educational, scholastic — an almost prophylactic or preventive point of view. He had conceived psychosynthesis as therapy for the healthy man, and in fact, as a means to maintain health psychosynthesis is unique. I have developed all of these aspects and, at his suggestion, I have also worked with highly gifted children who have problems in the same way as less gifted children. It was a subject that was very close to Assagioli's heart.

What aspect struck you in particular about Assagioli?

His great openness to all our suggestions, which he always accepted. For example, in Vienna I had learned many things about hypnosis and other techniques, and he was very interested in it and also used this knowledge and these methods, which are not psychosynthetic. He had a great capacity for synthesis, he was very open to all knowledge and this in some respects brings him closer to Jung. If Freud had had the same openness, there wouldn't have been all the separations that occurred: I think of Jung and Adler, for example. Assagioli did not have any counter-transference towards his students: if one of them left because he was opening up to other dimensions and experiences, Assagioli acquired information about this new interest, and he was enriched in turn. Another aspect that was very striking in him was his serenity, which he kept despite everything. This serenity was an almost Indian type of attitude — not in the sense of fatalism, but in the ability to make the best of every situation, always, even if it was negative. He saw the good wherever it was possible and developed this healthy part, this positivity that can be found everywhere. I make this comparison: sometimes psychoanalysis throws a lot of ballast down from the balloon to allow it to rise; psychosynthesis puts helium or hot air inside, and thus reaches very, very high goals using different systems. This does not negate the fact that the first part of psychosynthesis is analytical, even though it is not based so much on sexuality as Freudian analysis is.

What did the meeting with Assagioli mean for you, both personally and professionally?

I learned tolerance, availability, openness to any therapeutic method. I learned not to rely on pathology, but to also see the other side, the healthy part of man, which is substantial even when it does not seem so. Above all, what struck me and left deep traces in me was his "smiling wisdom," as he called it. One of the most important techniques of psychosynthesis, which we also find in Indian Vedanta, is that of disidentification from the various personalities that exist in us: I am here, I am this, but I am also other things, I am different, I will soon become such and such. I also learned from Assagioli the ability not to fasten myself to a single role; that is, if suddenly I had to do another job, I would have the humility to start over.

It seems to me that psychosynthesis is better known abroad than in Italy. Is this so?

It's true. He wrote his first book in English, and when I asked him the reason for this choice he replied that very few people know Italian and many know English, so he had used this language. That first book, which was later translated into Italian,[131] was a best-seller and made Assagioli known in America and other foreign countries.

Is psychosynthesis as a psychological technique followed by many therapists?

This is a question that requires a preliminary explanation. Psychosynthesis is so vast — and it can even be called "possibilistic" — that it has no precise rules; it is a therapeutic project more than anything. I think this is the greatest difficulty. Psychosynthesis provides many principles and exercises; however when one has practiced psychosynthesis, one becomes a *therapeutic self*, going beyond the mainstream, the Self, the oedipal complex and so on: one becomes a healer, a shaman. Psychosynthesis helps people to become "psychosynthesists," but nobody will ever become one as one becomes a psychoanalyst or a Jungian. Those who have really studied psychosynthesis understand that they can use various methods and techniques depending on the patient they have. The true follower of psychosynthesis is sufficiently evolved, has enough resonance, so that the other, the patient, is favorably affected by his presence. Psychosynthesis is therefore practiced by very few people. Those who do are advanced enough to be able to do anything, to be able to use any method, since they have digested everything in such a way as to resonate in a certain way. In fact, we find that different people practice

---

[131] *Psychosynthesis: A Manual of Principles and Techniques,* of which we have already spoken.

psychosynthesis in completely different ways. This is because there are no fixed rules, and because they have actually become healers. Psychosynthesis must be lived more than practiced. The important thing is to know your limits and never lose sight of the clinical aspect, which sometimes happens in other approaches. As a doctor and a clinician, I care about the results. So who is a psychosynthesist? In the end we all are, because it is a way of seeing ourselves. Of course, if one has followed a teaching, this is good. They say that I do psychosynthesis, and it is certainly true, but I do not notice it. I recognize that I have many faces and I try to harmonize them as much as possible, I try to disidentify myself, like Garibaldi who, having finished a task, returned to Caprera to sow the beans. [132]

Returning to the results: the therapist must accept all methods as long as they have a positive effect. This is the right clinical attitude. We need flexibility, tolerance, and have no desire to proselytize, which is something limiting. Proselytism is ultimately an act of insecurity, because it makes you feel protected and powerful. Assagioli did not want a "court," he was above these things: many people came, went, started, then changed their minds. He accepted and understood. I also behave like this, I do not hold on to anyone. More than a teaching, psychosynthesis is a way of being.

Psychosynthesis has given a lot to transpersonal psychology, hasn't it?

Transpersonal psychology took everything from Assagioli, and many people loyally recognize this. Still speaking as a clinician, as a doctor, in my opinion it is necessary to keep in mind all aspects of psychosynthesis, because it can be dangerous to jump directly into the transpersonal Self: it can be an escape. If there is not first a cure of the natural [or personal] self, of the very low, animal self, with its wants and needs, then it is not possible to make the leap to the top, because then it is without foundation.

Psychosynthesis is the Cinderella of psychology. Everyone has taken from her, developing various aspects, often forgetting the main root. The old trunk, which grew all these branches, has remained there, a little ignored and forgotten . . .

---

[132] *Guiseppe Garibaldi (1807-1882) was an Italian general, patriot and revolutionary whose military activities brought about the unification of Italy. When this work was accomplished, rather than claim some office for himself, he retired to the island of Caprera and refused to accept any reward for his services. —Ed.*

MASSIMO ROSSELLI
"Psychosynthesis is essentially a psychology for healthy people."

Dr. Massimo Rosselli (1943-2017) was a psychiatrist and psychotherapist who met Assagioli in 1966 when he was a medical student. He was a professor at the University of Florence, director of the Institute of Psychosynthesis in Florence, and was co-founder, vice-president and teacher at the Italian Society of Therapeutic Psychosynthesis. He worked in the area of psychosomatic medicine and edited various volumes, including *I nuovi paradigmi della psicologia* [*The New Paradigms of Psychology*], (1992), which brought together the works presented at the congress organized in Florence in 1988 on the occasion of the centenary of the birth of Roberto Assagioli.

How did you meet Dr. Assagioli? And how did your involvement with psychosynthesis come about?

> It was a gradual approach. I was a medical student and attended his lectures; little by little I approached his thought, and here I am!

In your opinion, is Assagioli known as he deserves?

> He is beginning to be known, but certainly not as he deserves, not in proportion to the wealth he left behind. Assagioli has sown a lot, and many seeds have been taken up — even by people who have not followed psychosynthesis. Others have followed it. There is a psychosynthetic movement in the air, a search for synthesis, but it must be said that Italy knows Assagioli relatively little. Perhaps the responsibility for this is to be attributed to its beginning in the psychoanalytic movement, from which it then detached itself. He was considered an outsider. He was a pioneer of the transpersonal — he began in the 1920s, even before Abraham Maslow. In America, Assagioli was recognized as one of the leaders of the transpersonal. He did not write much and compared to the way psychoanalysts and other teachers have spread their ideas, his influence has been in a limited circle. He preferred to work with small groups, or with individuals, privately. Assagioli was considered a bit of a heretic for his interest in the mystical, transpersonal aspects: psychoanalysis sees these aspects as a "foreign body," to be kept separate, and therefore Roberto Assagioli was considered someone who was now sailing towards foreign shores. However, these aspects are also important on a therapeutic

level. Among other things, Assagioli is very basic and informative, accessible even to a person with little cultural background: he did not speak only to scientists. His simplicity was downright disarming!

What is psychosynthesis for you?

Essentially a psychology for healthy people. Assagioli remained a psychiatrist, a clinician, and he treated serious patients, even psychotic patients. But he also helped people who came for personal growth. We carry on this double discourse. Even the public that attends our centers are of all kinds. Psychosynthesis has been running courses for people interested in their own growth since the 1960s. And this is a new, important aspect.

What did Assagioli leave you personally?

Over time my esteem grows. I appreciated him when he was alive, even if not fully. I reevaluated him much later, every day in my work. Assagioli is very present to me. He taught me to always be direct with people. He was joyful, full of humor, he always had a wonderful smile — those infinite, welcoming, radiant eyes that broke through any rigidity. He was always serene, his spirituality was always present: there would be a meditative moment, the one in which the spirituality was most intense, but he seemed to me to be in continuous meditation. Meeting with Assagioli gradually became important to me. When I was very young I was more critical, then over time his person magnetized me, he won me over more and more. Assagioli has left us a significant legacy to carry on. The countless notes, the insights he wrote . . . There is still much to discover, to understand. I remember with particular emotion the way he knew how to be welcoming to us young people, as he encouraged us, stimulated us. He was a man who left his mark — and those eyes that came from far away, infinite, smiling . . .

ANDREA BOCCONI
"Being able to get back on the road every moment."

Andrea Bocconi (1948-) is a psychologist and psychotherapist from Lucca who was one of Roberto Assagioli's youngest students. He graduated in law, but later practiced as a psychologist, to which he was introduced by Assagioli himself, and with whom he lived for long periods. He is a teaching member of the Italian Society of Therapeutic Psychosynthesis (SIPT) and senior instructor at the Stockholm Academy of Psychosynthesis. He has worked in various cultures, developing a competence in ethnopsychology. A Director and teacher of writing at the Scuola del Viaggio (School of Travel), he has been dealing with autobiographies in clinical practice for years. Among his published works are *Il Matto e il Mondo* [*The Fool and the World*] and *La mente e oltre Psicosintesi per educatori* [*The Mind and Beyond: Psychosynthesis for Educators*]. Andrea Bocconi preserves particularly significant memories of Assagioli.

When did you meet Assagioli?

> In late 1971. I had done my military service with Piero Ferrucci and we had become friends and I had acquired a certain interest in meditation. I talked about it with Piero and he, on his own initiative, made an appointment for me with Assagioli. I was embarrassed, I didn't know what to say to him. Instead, it was a very powerful meeting. I found myself talking at length about myself; he took me under his wing and invited me to come back whenever I wanted. At that time I was finishing my law studies and I wanted to be a judge of the juvenile court. Assagioli also supported me in this project. Then things took a different turn, because I realized that my orientation was moving towards psychosynthesis almost without my noticing it. Piero Ferrucci arranged for me to be Assagioli's secretary for a month, in the countryside in Capolona. My first reaction was not enthusiastic, however I went. In the beginning I had to make packages to send certain books to Florence and I, who had no manual skills, felt tied down and embarrassed. But after a while I realized that I was very happy, calm — in a word, I was fine. He gave me many books to read, there was secretarial work involving the Americans and the British who came to study with him, and we worked together. Little by little I got involved. At that time I had to prepare for my final law exam, which was particularly difficult and dry. He transformed the experience, explained to me that I could make it a yoga of patience. He told me many things that made me see the exam in another way. He was like that!

To what extent has Assagioli influenced your lifestyle choices?

To a considerable extent. I'll tell you a curious fact. Once I had gone to see him in Florence, he had cut out a piece of newspaper for me and had written on it, "For Andrea, a teaching competition." I never thought of dedicating myself to teaching. I wanted to be a psychotherapist, but with my law degree I felt a little embarrassed. Instead I attended a qualification course for teaching in social psychology, to which you could enroll with a law degree. And so I taught psychology in public school for fifteen years. It was a very beautiful, truly joyful experience, and I owe it to Assagioli. That fact made me realize that things happen at much more subtle levels than what I was used to thinking about. Now I only do therapy, although I have kept up with some activities in the wider field.

What do you remember of Assagioli?

His simplicity. I was intrigued to read his writings from when he was twenty years old, because compared to then he had "stripped down" in an incredible way. His path had gone from complexity to extraordinary simplicity. His books are simple, although not easy, because there is a great density: in half a page there are things that may require an entire evening to be developed. I remember his humor, the joyful aspect that was very strong in him. The quality of Self that he expressed most was joy, along with will. When I met him he was already 83 years old, he was a frail old man. The sessions with me lasted just fifteen minutes, because then he was tired. And he didn't write more than an hour at a time for the same reason. He had to pace himself a lot, but he retained his determination to a life of service until the end. There is a detail that I always remember: he had a small boat on his desk and when they dusted they often moved it. He always put it back in the direction of the window, towards the open space, and I once with the curiosity of a twenty year old asked him why. "Because for me it represents adventure," he replied, "I can travel every moment, change, question everything." For me this remains a reference point, because I wonder if I too would be willing to really question everything . . .

What was your relationship with Assagioli like?

Very affectionate. I could ask him anything. For example, one day I asked him if he knew when he was going to die, and he replied, "I have not been informed," as if I had asked him the most normal thing in the world. I felt a filial or even grandson relationship with him. He brought out special emotions in me; he always made me feel happy; he stimulated my creativity. He was a pioneer, he had always dedicated himself to others and continued to do so until a few days before he died. It was natural for him to help those in need. He was very generous, very kind, and he never asked for anything for himself. He had no attachment; if one chose another path he did not have any bad reaction. He showed us a lot of confidence: he quickly threw us into the fray, a bit with the haste of the old man who wants to put down the baton. In Florence there was no middle generation, because Bruno Caldironi was in Ravenna, and Sergio Bartoli was in Rome. So he engaged us very young and very early: I was 24 or 25 years old. He left our personal paths up to us, he supervised; his direct guidance at that time was mainly on the transpersonal side.

Do you remember any particular episode, characteristic of Assagioli?

There would be many, but what I will tell you seems very evocative. Once he was conducting a meditation in his study when one of the ladies who looked after him entered, without knocking, to ask him to choose the fabric for his pajamas. He chose, thanked the lady, and she left. He closed his eyes and started meditating again. I had experienced all this as an interruption, but for him it had been different: what had happened had not moved him a millimeter. He hadn't gotten bothered or upset. Besides, I never saw him angry or irritated. He was stable, very serene; he made disidentification his whole life, so he freed himself from emotions. When we "dinosaurs" of psychosynthesis meet, we who knew him and lived with him, we have the feeling that we met a special person once in a lifetime: we know we have had an authentic gift!

MATILDE SANTANDREA
"Man must be like the tree: rooted in the earth, but turned to the sky."

Matilde Santandrea (c.1926-) has a degree in literature and taught for several years at the University of Bologna, her home city. At the same time she cultivated her interest in psychology and followed the courses in psychosynthesis that Gabriello Cirenei, a friend and collaborator of Roberto Assagioli, held in Bologna. She met Assagioli in 1970 and became his pupil and then collaborator. For years she has devoted herself to dance therapy, and has created a special institute, "Chrysalis," to teach this technique. In this interview, she explained how and why her life has taken such a different direction.

When did you meet Roberto Assagioli?

> It was in 1970, when Assagioli invited me to call. In a card that I had prepared at the invitation of Gabriello Cirenei, with whom I had been studying psychosynthesis for two years, I had expressed my desire to teach psychosynthesis to others too, since it had done so much good for me. At the first meeting Assagioli told me this story: A young teacher had won a competition and had to go to teach in an unknown village in the mountains. He took his satchel with all his books and notes, but when he got to the village he couldn't find the school. He asked the children he met about it, but they knew nothing about it. Then he put all his papers and books aside, and went with the children to the woods and started building a school, cutting trees, making plans, building furniture, etc. At the end of the year he had taught nothing of what he had in mind to teach when he arrived in the country, but the children had built the school and knew how to count, organize themselves and do many things. When he was finished telling this story, Assagioli gave me a nice smile.
>
> I was amazed. I expected practical solutions, concrete suggestions on how to stand up for myself at school, because those years were very difficult and I taught big kids who were very argumentative. Assagioli showed appreciation for this and said that the students had finally woken up. I came from an old, traditional mentality, but he said that the student revolution was right. He had an incredible talent: one felt that what he said was the real thing, it was right. He shook my certainties with his statements: I changed my way of teaching and I gained many concrete benefits from it. The fable meant that you have to rebuild from the bottom, you have

to change, and not to do as you have always done. Assagioli had a great respect for the person, he gave suggestions, but never directly, and he never forced them to go in a certain way . . .

Did Assagioli help you undertake dance as a therapy?

Undoubtedly the push came from him, although always in his discreet, indirect way. I went to him regularly for four years. After some time with him he said to me, "You will do many things for my psychosynthesis!" I asked what, and he looked at me, smiling, and didn't answer. I never thought of developing the body aspect of psychosynthesis. Assagioli had said and written that movements and attitudes tend to arouse corresponding sensations and attitudes, and added that certain dances are the application of this principle. He also said very clearly that physical energies must always be involved. In fact, his system is *biopsychosynthesis*, although for brevity it is called *psychosynthesis*. "Never forget *bios*," Assagioli repeated. After a long time I understood that my path was precisely to develop this aspect. He had a great intuition and said to me, "You will do things you are not even aware of now." He saw the person projected into the future, and he understood that I would find my own way. In fact, I am very independent. I didn't think about dance at the time. I started thinking about it in 1978 following a dance course in Paris taught by a teacher from Findhorn.[133] It was not only a shock, but a disaster — because I was uncoordinated. Then there was a reaction [in me] and I started working with music and dance. Assagioli said that music has effects on the psyche that are still mysterious. The body, he said, is the physical part of the unconscious. Working on the unconscious through the body means introducing principles that do not come through reason. The symbol is the great transformer of consciousness, which the body brings to life intensely. Psychodance has the power to break through the bark that imprisons us; with dance the mind rests and the body works. Then comes the moment of discussion, of commenting on what dance has liberated.

---

[133] Findhorn is a community for the new consciousness, which arose in Scotland some thirty years ago under very special circumstances. Those interested in learning more can read the book *Findhorn* by Paola Giovetti. *This book was published in 1992 by Edizioni Mediteranee (currently out of print) and is available only in Italian. There are several books about Findhorn available in English, including* Flight into Freedom and Beyond: The Autobiography of the Co-Founder of the Findhorn Community, *by Eileen Caddy (2002).—Ed.*

Was Assagioli important to you also on a personal level, as well as a professional one?

Yes, very important. I did my personal psychosynthesis with him. I was desperate then: I was living with a schizophrenic husband, and Assagioli wanted to help me overcome this situation. He was a great support for me, he saved my life. I was really devastated — living with that kind of sick person is terrible. He knew how to help me very gently. With me, he started immediately with the superconscious, that was the right way to save me. When I came to him I melted into a river of tears even without him saying a word. I deeply felt the impact of a person who was different from all the others — he was peace, tranquility. As soon as I arrived he would take me to the window and say to me, "Let me see you, you always bring me joy. What a beautiful dress you have, what a beautiful color!" He had a sense of wonder that children have. This way of welcoming me comforted me and above all the trust that he was able to give me was good for me, even though I was not a psychologist and I was in that particular state of mind. He gave unconditional trust. He pushed me to give lessons on psychosynthesis here in Bologna. I did it for twelve years, then I opened *Chrysalis*, my center. I was reluctant to speak in public, but he said: "I agree that you are afraid, but don't let that hold you back!" In those last years he wanted to train students; he was in a hurry. He was able to create a collaborator in a few months, because it was the contact with him that worked the miracle. It gave me a sense of self-confidence that I didn't have at all!

Who was Assagioli?

An ancient sage living in modern times. Wise in the sense of simplicity: he put himself at our level, he gave great importance to the person. He spoke with great simplicity, but also with great authority. Once my family problem was discussed, he told me that sacrifice is the great law of life. I asked him if he was really sure about that, and he looked at me intently and replied, "*Very sure!*" I didn't accept these words then, and I couldn't put them into practice, because for me then sacrifice meant renunciation. Years later I understood that sacrifice is *giving* and I give lessons on this issue myself. I once went to him with my husband, who was seriously ill. Assagioli let him speak for an hour, and I was unable to interject, to tell him that Assagioli could not hear: in recent years he had become deaf. So for an hour my husband told him everything about himself. Assagioli put a hand on his shoulder and said to him, "Son, there was no love." He understood the meaning if not the words. My husband thawed, and later said that no one in the world had ever understood him as Assagioli did. An empathy had arisen between them through the way Assagioli looked at him. He consciously radiated with his gaze and said that the eyes are not only the mirror, but also the transmitters of the soul. He also said to us students that we had to learn to transmit with our eyes . . .

What was Assagioli for you?

He was father (I needed a positive father figure), guide, and teacher. And I continued to feel his influence even after his death — many things I understood only after 10 or 15 years. He gave short and profound answers, understandable according to the maturity of the person. Growing up and rethinking those answers, we discover something more. His books seem easy, even sometimes almost banal, then rereading them after years we discover profound things that we had not noticed before.

Among the many things that Assagioli expressed with his psychosynthesis, is there one that you particularly appreciate?

It incorporates every level: emotional, mental, spiritual. No level must be lost, and the upper one incorporates the lower one. Assagioli said that one should never forget the roots, and gave the example of the tree, which grows in height as it goes deeper. It needs the roots to go deep and the branches to expand in height. If you cut off its roots or deprive it of the light at the top, it no longer grows. The tree for Assagioli has always been the symbol of man: it must be rooted to the earth but turned to the sky. If you can be this way, you are truly in line with the principles of psychosynthesis.

VITTORIO ARZILLA
"For him, psychosynthesis was a service to humanity."

Mr. Arzilla was Administrative Secretary of the Institute of Psychosynthesis of Florence from 1968 to 1982. He knew Roberto Assagioli well, and worked with him for six years. He had very precise and interesting memories of the founder of psychosynthesis.

How did you become connected with the Institute of Psychosynthesis?

I was retired as a naval officer, and had returned from abroad and was tired of being idle. I read in the newspaper that the Institute, as a charitable institution, was looking for a secretary who knew English. I introduced myself, found Ida Palombi who immediately welcomed me and led me to Assagioli. He told me that the Institute was poor, and could not give me more than 75,000 lire a month.[134] I accepted because I wasn't interested in money; I wanted to do something intelligent and interesting. It was the day after Epiphany, and when he heard my words Assagioli said, *"Ida, he was sent to us by the Epiphany!"* I stayed there for 14 years, and had a very cordial relationship with everyone. I handled practical and administrative matters. There was a lot of confusion and it took me two years to get everything right.

So the Institute never had much money . . .

No. Assagioli was an idealist and he never exploited or let his collaborators exploit psychosynthesis — he always considered it a service to humanity. People from all over the world came here and the rate for everyone was 5,000 lire.[135] I was angry, because I knew the difficulties of the Institute well. True, it was the seventies, but 5,000 lire for a world-renowned professor like Assagioli was very little. He could have asked for at least 50,000. Not only that, he gave the 5,000 lire to those who had no money! Even though Assagioli was Jewish, he was not at all stingy;[136] he was generous. He was not a

---

[134] *This would convert to $120.00 in U.S. Dollars in 1968, according to The Pacific Exchange Rate Service list of currency rates 1950-2023. —Ed.*

[135] *This would convert to $8.00 in U.S. Dollars in 1968, and a little more in 1973. —Ed.*

[136] *According to a recent conversation with the author, this was meant jokingly. —Ed.*

practitioner, but he was registered on the list of Jewish Israelites in Florence, who have to pay a certain fee for the community, and he was heavily taxed.[137] Once he sent me to them to explain that he accepted only 5,000 lire from patients, so he was not rich.[138] His wife, who died a year before him, left everything she had to him, and he in turn left everything to the Institute.[139]

What kind of life did Roberto Assagioli lead?

When I met him he was already old. He led a fairly sedentary life, wrote a great deal but was very inactive; he moved reluctantly and every now and then I accompanied him for a short walk. He received people from all over the world; he was very friendly, he gave very well-attended conferences. In later years, the sessions with patients exhausted him because he was in fragile health. A curious aspect — he was quite self-conscious [about his appearance], and if a lady came he would apply some cologne. He had great sympathy for my wife, who once gave him a tie; he always wore it and was cremated wearing it.

What kind of man was he?

An idealist, deeply convinced of man's goodness. He said that there is a devil in man, but it can be overcome with goodwill. He believed a lot in the exercises he had people do, especially the rose exercise.

What did you learn from him?

Serenity, impartiality, and a sense of duty: after all, I am an officer, and it was not difficult for me to fit in. But I owe the serenity I have to him, it is he who brought it out in me!

---

[137] *Records indicate that the registration of Jews and the discriminatory laws against them that had been enacted by the fascist state in 1938 were abolished by the new Italian republican constitution in 1948. —Ed.*

[138] *There is no available information that Assagioli would have been subject to any special taxation either as a Jew or as a psychiatrist, however the taxation authorities may have assumed a certain level of income because of his professional status, since professionals were subject to a progressive taxation system. —Ed.*

[139] *Information gathered elsewhere suggests that this statement is not accurate. Assagioli left the villa at Via San Domenico in Florence and Villa Ilario in Capolona to the Institute; the rest of the estate was left to his niece, Donatella.—Ed.*

ADA CINI
"It was a joy to be with him that half hour a month!"

Ms. Ada Cini was a tenant of Roberto Assagioli from January of 1969. She was a widow with married children and lived alone. In 1995 she still lived in an apartment in the villa in Via San Domenico.

When did you meet Assagioli?

> Every month I went to him to pay the rent and he kept me talking for half an hour. He said he liked to chat with me because I was interested in many things. I was sorry I didn't have great learning, but he said that intelligence, and the desire to know, help people move forward. He was not only my landlord, he was a friend. It was an enormous satisfaction to be with him for half an hour and escape from everyday things!

What struck you about him?

> Many things. His willingness to talk about everything — he was very cultured and informed about everything. Every time I went to his studio I found a new card. This was something that struck me so much. For example, "serenity," "fortitude," and so on. Cards indicating values that must be cultivated. He said that life has an immense purpose and that even negative things can have a positive outcome. He encouraged people to learn to live rightly, to carry out daily life with serenity. That half hour per month was very important to me, and when I left I felt a great joy. He always suggested that I live in such a way as to prepare for future life. His was the figure of the prophet, even his physical figure was like that. He was a person who knew life and who wanted to instill in others that optimism, that serenity that no one teaches anymore. He was simple, but one could sense his greatness. It was a great teaching. When I came back from that half hour, I seemed to have understood many things. With him, paying the rent was a pleasure . . .

SUSANNE NOUVION
"The "I" must decrease, the Self must increase."

Ms. Nouvion (1907-1997) from Paris was the founder of the French Institute of Psychosynthesis. A teacher by training and very engaged in social and cultural initiatives, Susanne Nouvion met Assagioli in 1961 and studied with him assiduously for many years.

When did you meet Roberto Assagioli and what was the occasion?

> I met him in 1961 in Montreux, Switzerland, at a conference on psychosynthesis. I am a teacher, and with a friend I founded a call center in Paris, to provide telephone support and suicide prevention counseling, and also a center to help parents of young suicides, people who could not accept what happened and find peace. When we talked about these initiatives to Assagioli, he was enthusiastic; he said that we were on the same wavelength and that we were made to work together. He also added that what we were doing was already psychosynthesis. We became friends, and later in Florence he created something very similar to what we had done here in France.[140] Meanwhile, we were studying psychosynthesis: for years we went periodically to Florence or to Capolona to work with him and to follow the courses and conferences that he organized. He was keen to pass on his method, but in reality the method was himself: being with him, doing the meditations and the exercises was a great school. When Assagioli thought we were ready, he told us it was time to bring psychosynthesis to France. We founded the French Institute using the location of the Social Center that we had created years before. Psychosynthesis is followed with interest in France; Assagioli's thought is high quality, but accessible to many.

Which aspect of psychosynthesis has most affected you?

> The unity of being, and at the same time respect for all levels of being, from the most primitive to the highest. Psychosynthesis is a brilliant method precisely for this attention to energy capable of reawakening the light that is in

---

[140] It was mentioned by Ms. Tina Muzzi above.

every being and removing blockages, making man grow with his own strength. Psychosynthesis is spiritual and at the same time realistic and concrete; it works on the everyday level. If this were not so, it would not be so important.

What was Assagioli like as a person?

Cheerful and charming. He said many interesting things. He was paternal, infinitely respectful — he took care of everyone. He was an exceptional being: a true Master. I compare him to Teilhard de Chardin, I would put it at that level. Teilhard also impressed me a lot and I see an affinity between his thought and that of Assagioli. One thing that struck me about him was his physical frailty: he was a spiritual figure. He was as wise as he was modest, but with an intelligent modesty. I thank God that I met him.

Did you also meet his wife?

Of course, she was always present in Florence and was a very original woman, but nice and intelligent. They loved each other very much! She was involved in parapsychology; she also did sessions with mediums. He had an interest in esotericism, but he didn't tell us about it — what he cared about was psychosynthesis and we focused on this. Returning to his wife, they had a good emotional rapport; she respected him very much from every point of view. She did not have the preparation to follow him in his scientific work, but she gave him a lot of emotional support, which is an important thing.

What did you learn from Assagioli?

His was a striking personality: he was simple, cheerful, and full of spirit. He had no sense of self-possession, he lived modestly and asked very little or even nothing from those who came to him. He had no will for personal power, and repeated, "the 'I' must decrease, the Self must increase." He fully embodied his message in his person: his dialogue with the spirit was continuous. I especially remember his joy; after knowing him, one was no longer the same, not so much for what he said, as for how he was. He had a great love for people. Italy must be honored to have had a son like him.

In your opinion, has Assagioli contributed much to the development of psychology?

> He has given much to psychology, sociology, pedagogy and spirituality: he has included the spiritual level in psychology, and this is very important. He was a great universal spirit — he was Israelite, but he was also very Christian, in the sense that Christ was the true Messiah for him. He was very open and was the forerunner of transpersonal psychology, which owes him a lot. He provided many ideas that have not yet been fully understood: I think he will not be understood completely for many years . . .

PETER ROCHE DE COPPENS
"He transformed me with presence, not with words or actions."

Peter Roche De Coppens (1938-2012), psychologist, anthropologist and sociologist, was born in Switzerland but usually resided in the United States, where he was a university professor. He was the author of various books on sociology, esoteric Christianity, the New Age and the New Consciousness. At the beginning of the seventies he did his personal psychosynthesis with Roberto Assagioli, whom he remembered gratefully and with admiration.

How did you meet Roberto Assagioli?

> It was an extraordinary meeting. Years before, that is, in the fifties, when I was a student, I had spent some long periods in Florence and some friends had given me some handouts by Assagioli. But we had never met. The direct meeting took place many years later and it quickened me, made me more than I normally was. His presence had the same effect as that of Mother Teresa of Calcutta, whom I have had opportunity to meet a few times: it had the effect of a bomb, even if he didn't say much. At the first meeting I came with friends: we didn't say much, because he had a communication problem at the time — he was hardly able to hear anymore. But he gave me work to do, books to read. I was in Europe for the Christmas holidays and I read everything he had recommended to me at that time. Then I phoned him from Switzerland to have another appointment before leaving and I found out from the secretary that he had already set it up for me. I went back to Florence and he had a smiling, slightly sly and mischievous look. I asked

him who I could work with in the United States because I was passionate about psychosynthesis, and he replied, "I'll work with you." He put me to the test: few words, lots of work; that is the method of initiatory schools. I worked with him in the following years in Florence and Capolona: the theoretical and practical part, teaching, personal psychosynthesis. Once, in Capolona, he told me that by now he had little time left, and that therefore he would tell me things that he normally would not say. Usually he allowed things to mature in people by themselves, so that the person would become aware of the facts by himself. But that time he did: he described the basic mechanisms of my psyche with a lucidity, clarity, an incredible synthesis. He apologized for doing it so quickly, but his time was running out. He died a month and a half later.

What did Assagioli give you?

He gave me an impulse that I still feel, and that I have tried to integrate both in my courses and in my books. Every now and then I have the impression that he is close to me, I feel him next to me, I hear flashes that are typically his. Maybe it's my unconscious, but the subjective feeling is that he is present.

Is psychosynthesis known in the United States?

It has more resonance in the United States than in Italy, for various reasons. First, transpersonal and humanistic psychology are more alive in America than in Europe, and therefore Assagioli and his psychosynthesis, which has given both these movements so much, are often mentioned. Then in the United States the original contribution of psychosynthesis, which consists in introducing the spiritual dimension into psychology, is highly appreciated. With his exercises — autobiography, meditation etc. — psychosynthesis works on the crises that precede, accompany and follow spiritual awakening. At these three stages there is a temporary disorganization of the psyche which can also be misunderstood and possibly interpreted in a psychopathological way instead of in terms of personal growth. Assagioli's model of the psyche is the most holistic and advanced that we have: it includes the biopsychical and the spiritual part. For people who are interested in spiritual and religious life, in the awakening of the higher energies, psychosynthesis is a fantastic key, because it is simple, scientific and gives results. All of this is highly appreciated in America, and understanding of Assagioli is growing. No wonder it's a slow process: he was fifty years ahead of his time!

Among the various things that Assagioli said to you, is there one that struck you in a particular way?

I was very impressed by the story of the experience he had in Venice at 11 ½ years old. Looking at the setting sun, he received the intuition about the structure of the psyche and the mystery of the Self. All the basic ideas he had right then, in just 20 minutes. He said to me, "That day I received the skeleton of psychosynthesis, then all my life I put the flesh around that skeleton." At 11 years old he had already seen the personal and transpersonal Self!

Assagioli had many aspects: is there anyone who has known him completely?

He was a bottomless well of information and knowledge: those who met him saw some of his facets, but I don't think anyone saw them all.

What did he teach you?

To be simple but to go to the essentials; to be practical but effective; to find the connections between the parts and the whole. For him, the key to our era was to establish right relationships. André Malraux said that the 21st century will be spiritual or it will not *be*. For Assagioli, the 21st century was to be the century of right relationships that will create the New Age. Psychosynthesis is the science of conscious relationships: first of all within oneself (personal psychosynthesis); then there is the action between oneself and others (interpersonal psychosynthesis); between oneself and the Self (transpersonal psychosynthesis); and finally relationship between oneself and the world (cosmic psychosynthesis). It is a very broad vision. He said few things, but every word was measured, connected with other ideas and aimed at growth, and led the person to grow. I think everyone who knew him experienced growth. By doing personal psychosynthesis, I realized that I was growing on three levels simultaneously: that of knowledge, that of feeling and love and that of will — that is, understanding, feeling, acting. Assagioli made a mark on all those who studied with him. Being with him was an unforgettable thing. True masters have this common feature: when you are in their presence, your self grows and you come out transformed. It was his presence alone that does this, not the words, not the actions — the presence.

The most important thing that Assagioli gave you?

He revealed to me a part of myself that I didn't know, to which I aspired but that was unknown to me. And then he gave me a great desire to do things, to live, to experiment, to have adventures, to live life in the fullest sense. Perhaps the essential thing that he was able to convey was enthusiasm — that is, with a momentary process of tuning he was able to awaken your Self, the superconscious; to give a vision and a glimpse of what you could become; he also gave the impetus and life force to try to get there. He communicated to all who were with him that life was worth living, despite everything. He had had a very difficult life. Once he said to me, "At the bottom there are no solutions, at the top there are no problems" — that is, the key is never in the horizontal dimension, it is always in the vertical. But he stressed that it takes the union of vertical and horizontal, because if you get stuck horizontally, you have to go vertically, and when one has gone high enough vertically to find the light and the fire, one must go horizontally to live and embody the things that have been discovered — to make them come true, one must make them flow in the world. Another thing that he passed on to me was the understanding that all human experiences have a meaning, a purpose and a value. There is nothing that is negative, or indifferent, or spoiled; in any situation, you can always choose whether to stop or to grow.

You said before that you continue to feel Assagioli present; in what sense do you mean this?

I will try to explain. One thing that was typical of him (that was also typical of Padre Pio, Mother Teresa and people of that level) was that after you got to know him, a part of him always remained with you. That is, the meeting with people of this type does not take place over time, but *sub specie aeternitatis*: [141] it remains in you, as if the vibration of this person, his energy, entered you and left something indelible. When in my life I found myself with problems, I asked myself: what would Assagioli do if he were in my shoes, how would he

---

[141] *Latin: From an eternal perspective.* —Ed.

see this situation? And this has helped me enormously; it is a true exercise of disidentification, it means moving from one level to another. The situation remains the same, but you experience it in another way.

What, in your opinion, is the basic characteristic of psychosynthesis?

I believe that Assagioli's great work was to translate the perennial philosophy into modern and scientific terms, and to make it available to people of good will. One day I asked him to define the scientific method and he replied, "It is replacing authority and tradition with observation and direct experience." He had a great feeling for Mary and Martha[142] — he felt the dialectic between the two sisters, who were friends of Jesus: meditation, inner life, and realization; and then outer life, relationship and organization. He wanted to unite these two aspects in the right way, in order to achieve the great work; that is, the conscious union with the Self as the unifying principle that guides our life.

Do you remember any of his curious, particular statements?

Yes. For example, he cast horoscopes very well and greatly appreciated esoteric astrology, which provides a certain kind of self-knowledge, and the alchemy that provides self-control. He said that sooner or later these disciplines would be integrated into psychology, to enrich and complete it. He was a Renaissance man in the true sense of the word, with an infinite thirst for knowledge . . .

---

[142] "Mary and Martha" are in an episode in the life of Jesus related in Luke 10:38-42. Assagioli wrote a long monograph in Italian titled "Marta e Maria" that was published in the magazine Ultra_in 1922. He prepared a version in English titled "Martha and Mary: A Study of Outer and Inner Action" that was first published in the UK by Sundial House in 1966, revised in 1975. —Ed.

CHAPTER 4
THE LAST YEARS: LIBERATION

> I may die this evening but I would willingly accept a few more years in order to do the work I am interested in, which I think may be useful to others. I am, as the French say, *disponable* (available).
> —R. Assagioli, from the Interview with Sam Keen

THE FRUITFUL TIME OF OLD AGE

The last years of Roberto Assagioli's life were intense, fruitful and full of satisfaction. Even if his health left something to be desired and his physical frailty increased, the Maestro of Via San Domenico did not give up any of his activities: psychosynthesis spread throughout the world and he followed the path of his creation with love and anticipation.

In the 1950s he organized the first International Psychosynthesis Conference in Capolona with speakers from various countries. In 1958 the first important international milestone occurred; that is, the establishment of the Psychosynthesis Research Foundation in the United States, which Assagioli would visit several times.

Until a few years before his death Assagioli traveled extensively: he participated in conferences in Austria, France, Switzerland and England. He traveled to Tunbridge Wells, Kent (England) every summer for several years in a row to hold meditation courses.[143]

In 1966 the Biopsychosynthesis Center was founded in Argentina. The following year, 1967, as we saw in the interview with Dr. Sergio Bartoli, the Center was created in Rome, followed shortly by those in Bologna, Perugia and various others.

Also in 1967, Assagioli took part in the International Psychosomatic Week in Rome with an address on the theme "Psychosomatic Medicine and Biopsychosynthesis." He also chaired an international symposium on psychosynthesis. The following

---

[143] *Assagioli wrote an entire three-year course in meditation for the Meditation Group for the New Age. This material is used and available at both Sundial House in the UK and Mediation Mount in California, groups which were founded by Assagioli's associates. Other associated groups were founded in France, the Netherlands, Belgium, Italy, Spain, and Canada. —Ed.*

year, the Center in Rome organized the International Psychosynthesis Week, once again presided over by Assagioli.

Meanwhile, the psychosynthesis centers abroad were multiplying: India, Greece, California, Canada, London.

Assagioli's life was very intense. In addition to travel in Italy and abroad for meetings and conferences, there were psychosynthesis courses in Florence, consulting, teaching students and collaborators, and meetings with people of culture from all over the world. These were also the years in which Assagioli found those who would carry on the torch of psychosynthesis: Sergio Bartoli, Bruno Caldironi, Piero Ferrucci and many others that we have learned of through the interviews in the previous chapter.

Ida Palombi, the extraordinary secretary and collaborator who had taken the fortunes of psychosynthesis to heart and who would preside over the Institute after the death of its founder, watched over the smooth operation of the Institute in Via San Domenico.

In addition to everything we have already mentioned, Assagioli collaborated as a member of the editorial board of the *Journal of Humanistic Psychology* and the *Journal of Transpersonal Psychology*, organs of the two respective psychological currents to which Assagioli had contributed so much. An intense activity that would tire a young and healthy man — and Roberto Assagioli was no longer either.

Family life flowed on serene tracks. Winter and mid-seasons in Florence, summer and part of autumn in Capolona at Villa Ilario, the small villa built after the death of his son. Occasionally they took a different holiday, suggested by Assagioli's health conditions. We are informed once again by Ms. Luisa Lunelli, from whose essay we have drawn several times: a delightful picture of family life that deserves to be reported in its entirety.

> The doctors advised the sea for Roberto. Nella did not do well at the sea, but she wanted to accompany her husband to the sea every year. That year they invited me to spend July with them on the Tyrrhenian Sea. Ever since she had the experience of an exceptional summer storm that had suddenly dropped the temperature and brought the flu to Roberto, Nella had become extraordinarily foresighted and put shawls and pullovers in her luggage — coats also, I believe. By now she knew that in the rented apartments there is a shortage of kitchen utensils and dining room amenities, so she also packed pots and plates. Roberto, with the same foresight as his wife, was preoccupied with the work he could do on vacation, filling boxes of papers

and packing books, typewriter, and stationery. All this preparation began two months in advance, during which suitcases and parcels were deposited at the entrance of the apartment, which could thus give the air of a family preparing to emigrate.

On the day of departure, despite the large car they hired, it was not easy to arrange everything. Roberto, who had his share of responsibility, confined himself to being the "observer" and commented wisely from this privileged point of view, provoking laughter. When everything seemed settled, Nella and Roberto reached their places through narrow passages, but each one was tenaciously carrying a large personal bag. There were also the mutt dog and the Siamese cat: they were the representatives of the "Third Kingdom" in the family, as Roberto said, and they also went on vacation. It was quite difficult to get them to accept the places specially created for them. Once this was accomplished with caresses and tidbits, finally the departure took place amid the festive good wishes and the loud clapping of those who had helped . . .

Ms. Lunelli, who joined her friends by train a few days later, also tells how the days at the beach were spent:

The apartment was on the coast road, so that you only had to cross the road to the soft beach. It was a long stretch of beach that we crossed slowly, at Roberto's limping pace (Assagioli suffered from synovitis and had to use his cane), but he was happy. Carmela followed us with the deck chair, the shawl and the cushions. A short distance from the sea an open beach umbrella was waiting for us.

We sat Roberto down, we placed the pillow behind his back and the shawl on his lap. But he absolutely didn't want us to stay to keep him company; he insisted that we take a walk along the sea. And then, after making sure that he had his book, the newspaper and his glasses, we went down to the shore and began our walk, enjoying the coolness of the ripples that came to lap at our feet.

We walked, and every now and then we looked back to see him among the swimmers, and that was possible then, since the beach was not as crowded as the beaches of today. We went as far as we wanted to and turned around. Still walking along the sea, we again came even with our umbrella. We stopped and I caught Roberto's attention by waving my sun hat. He replied, waving the newspaper and gesturing with his arm and hand to go on: he didn't want our walk to be interrupted.

And we went on, talking about things we already knew, but we loved to repeat them to each other, like two sisters who loved to look over family things to imprint them in our minds better and better. We also spoke of Ilario, serenely, and of the impression he had left on those who had known him . . . And so on, until we went back to Roberto when the sun was setting and the tide came in. The afternoon at the beach was over. We helped Roberto get up and started going back. With the view of the sea in our eyes and its healthy breeze in our lungs, we made our way home step by step. Dinner and the quiet end of a day of harmony and peace awaited us . . .

These were generally peaceful years, even though Assagioli's health was declining over time. There was a case of flu that degenerated into pneumonia that nearly took him away, and there was the prostate surgery with the episode told by Dr. Piero Ferrucci in his interview. Ms. Angela La Sala Batà of Rome, already mentioned several times, told me that she had learned from Ida Palombi that in that moment of post-anesthesia half-sleep Assagioli had seen a "Master" who had proposed an "extension" to him if he would write books.

In fact, when he recovered, Assagioli wrote *The Act of Will* in English, which is the only book which he planned and created as such. The others are mainly collections of essays and lectures. Finally, it should not be forgotten that in the last years of his life Assagioli trained the students of the last generation and his psychosynthesis received the acknowledgments mentioned above.

ROBERTO ASSAGIOLI ALONE

Then came the difficult times of Nella's illness, which manifested itself with anxiety, a desire not to leave the house, loss of memory, and a gradual growing inability to recognize people: a degenerative illness that created significant caregiving problems. Roberto Assagioli never considered hospitalizing his wife in a clinic, and the whole family *ménage* was reorganized for the benefit of the patient. Faithful Carmela, daughter of one of Nella's tenants, ran the household. She lived with the Assagioli family in Via San Domenico for years, and after Nella's death stayed on to serve and assist Roberto.

THE LAST YEARS: LIBERATION

In 1972, although Nella was very ill, their golden wedding anniversary was celebrated. Carmela prepared a cake and Roberto recited a poem by Trilussa[144] that talks about being together in joy and pain.

Then, in 1973, Roberto was left alone.

We know that he had lost his hearing in his last days; he did not regret it, rather he joked about it, but certainly this limitation created problems.

He remained calm and active until the last. In May 1974, three months before he died, Assagioli dictated notes in English on "Training in Psychosynthesis;" they are published in a booklet of the Institute of Psychosynthesis also containing its statutes, and still constitute the basic elements of psychosynthetic basic training.

It is known that Assagioli had been working on a book on the theme that was most dear to him, *Height Psychology and the Self*, in which he intended to bring together in a systematic and organic way everything that in his long life he had intuited, experienced, and collected in this field. The project was not completed, but the book still saw the light. On the centenary of his birth, 1988, *Transpersonal Development*, edited by Maria Luisa Girelli Macchia in Rome, was released at the Astrolabio Publishing House,[145] and it gave some order to the notes Assagioli had been accumulating along with some of his other studies and essays on the same topic.

In the last period of his life Assagioli gave an extraordinary interview with the American philosopher, university professor and journalist Sam Keen.[146] Sam Keen had come to Florence in the spring of 1974 specifically to meet Assagioli, and described him and his living and working environment as best he could:

> Assagioli's office is a small room in his apartment, which is above the headquarters of the Institute. Books line two of the walls: Ralph Waldo Emerson, Herman Keyserling, Abraham Maslow and Carl Gustav Jung seem to be favorites. On the next to the bottom shelf *Jonathan Livingston Seagull* is perched between Rollo May and Erik Erikson. The desk is antique and covered with objects and papers (talismans of the shaman), fresh cut flowers (like tiger lilies I knew in Tennessee); a barometer; a clock; a kitchen timer;

---

[144] *Carlo Alberto Salustri (1871 - 1950) was an Italian poet, better known by his pen name of Trilussa (an anagram of his surname, "Salustri"). —Ed.*

[145] *Two translations of this book into English have been published, the most recent being by Inner Way Productions in Scotland in 2007. —Ed.*

[146] Published by the Centro Studi di Psicosintesi "R. Assagioli" of Florence. *This interview was originally published in English as "The Golden Mean of Roberto Assagioli" in the December 1974 issue of* Psychology Today. *Quotations here are taken directly from the English original. —Ed.*

scales; a flag of the United Nations; a star globe; two word-cards — ENERGY and GOOD-WILL. The walls, once white, have now yellowed like old bones. A stuffed Victorian love seat squats in one corner of the room.

Assagioli rises to greet me. He is old, fine-boned and frail, but the liveliness and delight in his face make his presence vigorous. His pointed goatee and salmon-colored-velvet smoking jacket lend an air of old-world authority.

Answering the first of the questions that Sam Keen had to write to him on paper due to deafness ("What are the major differences between psychosynthesis and psychoanalysis?") Assagioli presents the basic concepts of his psychosynthesis very precisely and concisely:

> We pay far more attention to the higher unconscious and to the development of the transpersonal self. In one of his letters Freud said, "I am interested only in the basement of the human being." Psychosynthesis is interested in the whole building. We try to build an elevator which will allow a person access to every level of his personality. After all, a building with only a basement is very limited. We want to open up the terrace where you can sunbathe or look at the stars. Our concern is the synthesis of all areas of the personality. That means psychosynthesis is holistic, global and inclusive. It is not against psychoanalysis or even behavior modification but it insists that the needs for meaning, for higher values, for a spiritual life, are as real as biological or social needs.

Words in which all of Assagioli is found with the deeper meaning of psychosynthesis. From this long interview by Sam Keen I quote Assagioli's last response. Keen asked him how he dealt with the idea of death, and he said beautiful and profound things, which express the convictions of a whole life and fully highlight the serenity, balance, and trust of the man Roberto Assagioli. Here is his answer:

> Death looks to me primarily like a vacation There are many hypotheses about death and the idea of reincarnation seems the most sensible to me. I have no direct knowledge about reincarnation but my belief puts me in good company with hundreds of millions of Eastern people, with the Buddha, and many others in the West. Death is a normal part of a biological cycle. It is my body that dies and not all of me. So I don't care much. I may die this evening but I would willingly accept a few more years in order to do the work I am interested in, which I think may be useful to others. I am, as the French say,

disponable (available). Also humor helps, and a sense of proportion. I am one individual on a small planet in a little solar system in one of the galaxies.

Commenting on these last words, Sam Keen adds that "in speaking of death there was no change in the tone or intensity of Assagioli's voice and the light still played in his dark eyes, and his mouth was never far from a smile."

LIBERATION

"Roberto lived the day of his Liberation." With these words the news of Assagioli's death, which occurred on August 23, 1974 in the quiet countryside of Capolona, at Villa Ilario, was announced to his friends. Assagioli had turned 86 some months earlier.

Professor Bruno Caldironi from Ravenna, recounted the last hours of the Master: "One evening Ida Palombi called me saying that the doctor was ill. I called Ferioli and Peresson, who lived near me, we met and together we reached Capolona. There we found Alberti, Rosselli and other students. He was already in a coma; I don't know if he recognized me. As an older student and neurologist, I was given the task of examining him: he had had a very severe stroke. When I arrived he was very agitated, but then he calmed down. He died peacefully in my arms."

Ida Palombi said that the last word that Assagioli spoke before losing consciousness was "Ilario," the name of his son. It was a relatively rapid transition, without prolonged suffering: a moment for which Assagioli, as we have seen, had long been prepared.

Roberto Assagioli's body was cremated on a wooden pyre in Arezzo on 30 August; the urn with its ashes was brought to the cemetery in Florence and placed next to that of his mother.

"Assagioli was inclined to believe in reincarnation," says Professor Bruno Caldironi again, "and according to this doctrine, burning the body makes it possible for the surviving spiritual component to detach itself more easily from the physical world."

Thus ended the earthly parable. The path of psychosynthesis has continued, entrusted to the disciples whom Assagioli had trained and who since then, with love and dedication, each following their own natural tendencies and grasping the most congenial aspects of psychosynthesis, have — to use the Master's own words — "watered the good plant."

CHAPTER 5
Smiling Wisdom

"If the dictators, big and small, and everyone in charge,
had good humor, this could help avoid wars!"
(*To Live Better*, page 23).

"Wisdom is an eternal smile."
(Archivio Assagioli, Florence)

Although St. Francis suffered much, he was happy and encouraged happiness in his friars. He used to tell them that they must be "God's jesters," in order to draw souls to God. In fact joy, gladness, and cheerfulness are magnetic.

These words[147] that Roberto Assagioli wrote about Saint Francis, a saint for whom he had a great admiration, certainly apply also to him. "Smiling wisdom" was truly the dominant note of his personality: all those who knew him bear witness to this, remembering with particular emotion his smile, his joy, his serenity, his ability to understand, accept, welcome, and help despite the many problems that life presented.

And it is precisely by emphasizing this aspect that I will begin to relate Assagioli's thought: a narrative that will necessarily be limited and partial, as his thought is very vast, ranging in all possible fields, and his writings — both what has been published and not published — are numerous. Moreover, this book is not intended as a text for specialists, but as a contribution to a better knowledge of Roberto Assagioli the man, about whom little has been written so far. But since Assagioli the man was, in everyone's opinion, the best expression of his psychosynthesis and he fully embodied it, I hope that my work — intentionally simple and readable for everyone — will be of some use even as a first approach to his psychology.

---

[147] Taken from the essay "Per Vivere Meglio" ["To Live Better,"] published by the Institute of Psychosynthesis in Florence. *The English version used here is taken from the Psychosynthesis Research Foundation PRF Issue No. 33 (1973), p. 17. —Ed.*

To recount the "smiling wisdom" of the father of psychosynthesis, I will use Assagioli's own words, quoting passages from various works and making extensive use of the many notes that have been organized after his death by Piero Ferrucci.[148] As I have already written, I was able to study them thanks to the courtesy of the Psychosynthesis Institute of Florence.

The Archive notes are precious thoughts, written by hand with a beautiful, clear nineteenth-century calligraphy, often on tiny sheets of paper — sudden ideas jotted down, intuitions, or projects — that allow a privileged, and partly unpublished, approach to Assagioli's thought. They have the great beauty of being quick, incisive, discursive, immediate and therefore very effective. In addition to this archival material that I will mark with (A), I will use passages from some other texts, in particular the booklet "Per Vivere Meglio" ["To Live Better"], which contains three essays entitled respectively "Life as a Game and Stage Performance," "The Technique of Cheerfulness," and "Smiling Wisdom" which I will mark with (V),[149] and the text "Educare l'uomo domani ["Educating Man for Tomorrow"] (E), which was created from the archive notes on the theme of education on the centenary of the birth of Assagioli (1988).[150] Both of these small books have been published by the Institute of Psychosynthesis in Florence.

This will be a personal approach, probably not very "technical," but I have confidence that it will be useful for a purpose which seems to me to be very close to Assagioli's heart: the growth of the individual, the understanding of his place and his role in the world, the serene and active acceptance of what life offers.

How should life be approached? Assagioli explains it with a highly effective phrase: Usually in life "one lets oneself live," while living is an art and should be the greatest of the fine arts. (V. page 3).

His great respect for life made him choose and emphasize with special attention this saying by Inayat Khan,[151] which expresses the importance of an always positive attitude towards what life offers: "He who look at life with horror is below

---

[148] *The work of the Assagioli Archives has continued thanks to the efforts of many volunteers. See https://www.archivioassagioli.org/index.php. —Ed.*

[149] *"Life as a Game and Stage Performance" and "Cheerfulness" were published in English as PRF Issue No.33 by the Psychosynthesis Research Foundation in New York in 1973; "Smiling Wisdom" first appeared in* Culture in the World *in 1946, and was republished by the Psychosynthesis Research Foundation.—Ed.*

[150] *This essay has not been translated into English as of this date. —Ed.*

[151] *Inayat Khan Rehmat Khan (1882-1927) was a poet, musician, philosopher, author, and pioneer of the transmission of Sufism to the West. He established the Sufi Order in London in 1914.—Ed.*

life; he who takes life seriously is within life; he who smiles at life with a happy smile, rises above the world." (V. page 21).

How can we correctly approach the things of the world, work, duties, commitments? Assagioli was rightly convinced that only by improving the individual is it possible to improve society, because a mature, committed, serene person necessarily ends up positively influencing those who are close to them in their emotional, social and work life. Hence his attention to the formation of the individual, to the interpersonal relationship. Assagioli knew that it is important to live well, to understand the profound meaning of the things of the world and events, to have values and set goals, and to express the opportunity to become "collaborators with God on earth," he retold a parable titled "The Three Stonecutters:" it is very eloquent and is accompanied by a brief, incisive comment by Assagioli himself:

> A visitor to the site of where one of the medieval cathedrals was being built asked a stonemason what he was doing. "Don't you see," replied the latter sourly, "I'm cutting stones," thus showing his dislike of what he regarded as unpleasant and valueless work. The visitor passed on and put the same question to another stonemason. "I'm earning a living for myself and my family," replied the workman in an even tempered way that reflected a certain satisfaction. Further on, the visitor stopped by a third stonecutter and asked him: "And what are *you* doing?." This third stonecutter replied joyously: "I am building a cathedral." He had grasped the significance and purpose of his labor; he was aware that his humble work was as necessary as the architect's, and in a certain sense it carried equal value. Therefore he was performing his work not only willingly, but with enthusiasm.

That is the parable. And here are Assagioli's comments:

> Let us remember the example of the wise workman. Let us recognize and always be aware that, however limited our ability may seem, however modest and humble our duties, in reality we are particles of the Great Life. We are participating in the unfolding of the Cosmic Plan, we are "collaborating with God." This recognition will enable us to accept every situation, fulfill every task, willingly, and with cheerfulness. (V. page 24).[152]

---

[152] *From "Cheerfulness," op.cit. —Ed.*

Assagioli, who was very attentive to the problem of young people and their education, suggested applying this parable directly to the students. In *Educating Man for Tomorrow* (page 88), we find an example of this application to a university student:

"What are you doing?"
1) I am preparing for an exam.
2) I am studying a science that I like.
3) I am preparing to create a better world.

"Creating a better world." This is the ultimate goal of psychosynthesis, which turns its attention to the personal as well as the social.

To live in the right way and "achieve our true place in the universe," says Assagioli, balance and sense of proportion are necessary. To obtain them, he suggested a meditation, an Eastern technique to which he often turned and which, when directed at different subjects, he considered a very useful exercise. We have seen in the biographical section that the practice of meditation was a daily custom for Assagioli. Here is the text:

Realization of our true place in the universe.
Let us gather in silence and let ourselves be pervaded by the infinite greatness of the universe, by the amplitude of its rhythms; let us feel like small particles of it, similar to myriads of other particles, one of the millions of inhabitants of a small globe, in turn one of the millions of other globes. By entering into this meditation, the "Copernican revolution" takes place within us, little by little, or sometimes suddenly. We no longer feel like the center of the universe; the right proportions are established between it and us. Yet, in a curious psychological paradox, instead of feeling diminished and humiliated, we almost feel a sense of expansion, of new dignity; and losing our false sense of importance, the presumption of pride and personal merits, we feel the value of the universe in us and we have the appropriate pride in being aware of it: that pride that makes Pascal say, "Man is a weak reed, but a reed that thinks." From this meditation we return to the labors of ordinary life more serene, better, with a clearer vision even for practical problems. And the echo remains in us and helps us in difficult and painful moments.

It is easy to do this exercise in the midst of nature; especially on the sea shore, atop a high peak, or contemplating the starry sky. Perhaps one of the reasons for the fascination of mountaineering, one of the motives attempting the peaks, lies in the desire to experience or to renew those states of mind.

When there is no opportunity for contact with nature, more indirect help can be used: readings in astronomy, geology, or the history of remote civilizations can distract us from personal concerns and can make us feel the immensity of life. (A)

And then Assagioli adds, "You don't even need to go outside, contemplate the entire sky. Even a single star seen through prison bars can touch a heart, awaken a soul." (A)

This, in all probability, comes from personal experience. Assagioli had been in prison and it is conceivable that viewing a small portion of the sky through the bars was beneficial for him as well.

To develop a sense of balance and avoid unnecessary self-pity, which unfortunately is very frequent even in apparently serene people, Assagioli suggests other reflections of great wisdom:

To combat self-pity, discontent, and material needs, vividly imagine the conditions of those who are worse off, of those who are in conditions of serious discomfort: in hospitals, asylums, prisons, concentration camps, etc. And also: sailors, fishermen at sea, coal stokers on ships, postmen in the mountains, employees in certain offices, etc. Help yourself with readings and pictures. (A)

The state of mind opposite from self-pity and discontent is good humor, joy, and serenity. Several writings by Assagioli are dedicated to these feelings, which can be sought and found with goodwill and also with exercises that can be performed by everyone. In the archives we find many notes dedicated to joy. Here are a few:

Joy is a spiritual coffee!
Joy vivifies, heals, radiates, arouses, activates.
Joy eliminates self-pity, criticism. Joy redeems.

And then a truly "joyful" list:

Effects of joy:

a. It enlivens, gives strength
b. It "de-fogs" emotional illusions, gives clear vision
c. It eliminates self-pity and depression
d. It eliminates fear
e. It eliminates criticism
f. It helps communion with the soul and the soul's action on the personality
g. It is in tune with the note of the Solar Logos
h. It makes [personal] irradiation powerful. (A)

Together with joy, Assagioli suggested cultivating humor, a quality with which he himself was amply gifted and which, in his judgment, can be reawakened within oneself. The extraordinary effects of humor are described in this evocative and engaging way:

What Giuseppe Zucca has so called the "steel cabin" of the self[153] cannot long resist — however hard and thick its walls may be —the subtle but penetrating and consuming flame of humor; sooner or later its door opens and man can free himself from that narrow and suffocating prison. When that happens, one can say that the greatest achievement has been reached. The soul spreads its wings and joyfully, with a divine smile, unites itself with the other souls, with all creatures and with God. (V. p. 33).[154]

And here is another very significant note on humor from the archive, which would be appropriate to meditate on and make our own, given that we live in a time full of tension, anxiety, and stress:

One of the difficulties . . . is the excessive tension in which we live.
How to remedy it?
One of the most effective and relatively easy means is humor.
True humor is spiritual. It involves:
    detachment
    comprehension
    benevolence, compassion
    inner freedom, spiritual elevation

---

[153] *Zucca used this metaphor in a poem titled "I" in a book of poems of the same name published in Rome in 1919.—Ed.*

[154] *from "Smiling Wisdom," op.cit. —Ed.*

SMILING WISDOM

    a sense of proportion
    a sense of rest.

How to use it?
First and foremost towards ourselves,
that is, towards our personality.
- — Play down our personal life
- — Learn to smile while suffering
- — Doing so sweetens the suffering, removes the sourness and bitterness that accentuate and complicate it
- — It lubricates the mechanism!

To others — especially towards those who are hostile to us and whose behavior tends to irritate us.
Better to smile than to be hostile.
Always remember the soul behind the small personality — both ours and others.
Of course, the humorous attitude doesn't have to be continuous, just a pause.
One must be serious when it is necessary, indeed more than we usually are, but reserve the seriousness, the fire, the energy for the things that truly deserve it, which are worthy of it.
If we squander our seriousness in small things, there is not enough left for the big ones! (A)[155]

And then a paragraph of rare effectiveness to describe the true nature of humor, a priceless quality:

True humor does not lie so much *being witty* as about bringing out the humor that is already *inherent* in facts and situations. Life often has humorous aspects; therefore God is the first and the greatest humorist. This is an attribute of God which is not found in theological treatises, but which is undeniable. Otherwise a humorist would possess a faculty that God would not have — which is absurd, since in this man would be superior to God! (A)[156]

---

[155] *Archive Doc. #12354, which is in Italian.* —Ed.

[156] *Archive Doc. #12352, also in Italian.* —Ed.

The risk, with reference to humor, is of abusing it; and here Assagioli warns against this danger:

> Humor, wit, is a condiment, a "salt" which should be taken in small doses. It does not nourish or give substance; it gives "taste" to food, it makes it "digestible" when it is "heavy." So it's good. Don't abuse it. Abusing it spoils the palate and the stomach, so that it has a bad effect and takes away the taste for healthy fruits that do not need "salt." (A)

Along with joy and good mood, humor should not be without laughter: it is a precious "medicine," and an "art" to be cultivated. Assagioli has dedicated several pages to laughter, from which we quote some passages:

> The ancients greatly appreciated laughter, which they looked upon as a divine gift and a helpful remedy. There never was a time when such a remedy was more needed than now. Men today are tense, agitated, frantic. They are driven by the passion for speed, the thirst for possessions and for conquest and thereby become exhausted. While not renouncing what is dynamic, constructive and heroic in our age, we should correct its excesses, moderate and balance its extreme tendencies.
>
> There are, above all, three things which modern man must learn in order to become a sane and complete being: *the art of resting, the art of contemplation, the art of laughing and smiling.* (V. p. 25)[157]

And again, in the same essay:

> Laughter removes the inner tension with consequent great relief to the individual; it brings with it a beneficent release and replaces the activity of tired functions by the fresh use of others which had been little — too little — employed. When one is tired or excited, it is easier to relax through laughter than through outer inactivity, during which the mind continues to pursue "in the void" its feverish activity.[158]

---

[157] *from "Smiling Wisdom," op.cit.* —Ed.

[158] *Ibid.*

Laughter produces another beneficial effect, says Assagioli: it makes man capable of playing again. Too soon we unlearn it, but this repression can be harmful to our mental health:

> Too early and too harshly do we repress "the little child" which dwells in us with its fresh gaiety and its need for free and happy playing. But this urge to play can be reawakened; it can bloom once more and exhilarate us, like a stream of fresh and pure water that issues from a mountain crevice. (V page 26).[159]

The playful attitude, understood in the highest sense of the term, was highly appreciated by Assagioli, who reported this biblical saying in one of his notes to himself:

> *Deus ludit in orbe terrarum* — God plays in the world.

And in another note he copied this sentence from Edison:

> I never worked in my life; it was all play! (V. p. 16)

To educators he recalls Plato's words:

> You don't start children to studying subjects by force of compulsion, but as if they were playing, so that you can also discover better the natural inclinations of each one. (A)

And with reference to the present time and the people of today:

> Don't take our personality too seriously. Play with our selves! (A)

And again:

> Let the child in us play (with awareness and balance). (A)

Man, on the other hand, tends to complicate existence with his own hands, and at the same time rejects the difficulties that life can present him. With fine humor

---

[159] *Ibid.*

and great intuition Assagioli notes this trend and with his usual discretion suggests a very different attitude:

> When he has no real problems to solve, man creates a quantity of artificial, fictitious, useless ones for the sake of solving them (for example, crosswords). This shows that man does not know how to live without problems. It is not right then to complain that God creates so many for us! At least His make more "sense" and are more useful! (A)

With regard to life and the problems it poses, Assagioli suggested an active, dynamic attitude, which seems best expressed in a phrase by Henry Ford, the great car manufacturer:

> *Don't find fault, find remedies; anyone can complain!* (V. page 16).

To evoke good feelings, serenity, patience, good humor, courage and so on, Roberto Assagioli suggested various techniques: meditations, guided visualizations, and real psychological training, some examples of which will be found in the next chapter. Here I would like to recall the "Technique of Evocative Words," which Assagioli defined as "symbols of the power of ideas," and which he personally used extensively. The people who knew him well remember those cards with the words "serenity," "patience," "joy," "courage," etc., which Assagioli alternated according to the mood he wanted to evoke or strengthen. As I wrote in the introduction, in his study you can still see two of these cards, probably the last ones he used in his house in Florence.

In the archive, in the folder of the same name, there are explanations of the Evocative Words and instructions for using them to the fullest: a very simple technique that everyone can personally experience by checking the results. Roberto Assagioli, who for years and years made constant use of the famous cards, speaks of it in these terms:

> Among the numerous techniques by which we can act on our psyche, and on that of others, in order to modify and even transform them, there is a very simple one that is easy to apply, yet very effective: the use of evocative words. This technique is based on well-established facts of psychic life and on the laws which regulate it, which have certainly been demonstrated. The fundamental fact is that of the receptivity and flexibility or malleability of our psyche. It can

be compared to a practically inexhaustible series of clear photographic films that are continually "exposed" by internal and external stimuli.

On this occasion we will deal only with external stimuli. The impressions that come to us from the environment in which we live exert a strong influence on the psyche, modify it and condition it continuously, and very often in a harmful way. Using another analogy, we can say that we live in a climate, in a poisoned psychic atmosphere and that we are constantly contaminated by it. This does not need to be demonstrated: contemporary life gives us evident and often dramatic evidence. Yet we expose ourselves and others to influences with such unconsciousness and passivity that truly such a civilization will in the future be considered inconceivable, almost "a psychological stone age."

Yet effective and easy-to-use means exist, both to protect against those harmful influences and to neutralize their effects. One of these consists in consciously evoking beneficial and constructive stimuli and influences. (A)[160]

Assagioli undoubtedly believed that evocative words exercised "beneficial and constructive" influences, whose efficacy was certain, in his opinion: they are symbols that express the "power of the ideas" that they represent, and as such they tend to produce the corresponding state of mind. By prominently placing a card on which the word of interest is printed, so that the eye often spontaneously falls on it, the image ends up impressing itself on the psyche, "more precisely in our plastic unconscious," and works silently but effectively.

Assagioli adds that it is also appropriate to meditate on the various evocative words, reflecting on their meaning and trying to "feel" their psychic quality, until one identifies with it. The choice of words to use is important, and it can be done either deliberately or by drawing lots, as "watchwords" for the day or for a certain period of time. Roberto Assagioli's "smiling wisdom" could not have devised a simpler and affordable tool for everyone to beneficially influence the psyches of people of good will.

Sam Keen, in his interview, asked Assagioli a question about the evocative words and, having received the answer, he wondered whether it was a simplistic or intelligent use of the automatic reactions of the body-mind. He could not answer, but made a "confession;" one evening he had placed a card with "joy" written on it in his hotel room in Florence, and waited for the results. The next morning he woke up with the room flooded with light and the sound of bells, with Italian coffee and Leonardo da Vinci in mind, and in a mood certainly marked by joy.

---

[160] *Archive Doc. #12754.* —Ed.

Power of suggestion? Once again Sam Keen leaves the discussion open, but his is undoubtedly an invitation to directly experiment with this simple technique suggested by the elderly, wise master of Via San Domenico.

The ultimate aim of Roberto Assagioli's psychosynthesis is the growth and inner enrichment of the individual. In the archive, under the title "Psychological Mountain Climbing," we find this beautiful phrase in English:

> If we dedicated to the psychospiritual ascent the same amount of thought, discipline, time, energy, money, enthusiasm, "asceticism" which is given by mountain climbers to a peak in the Himalayas...![161]

Instead, he notes that this is unfortunately rarely done:

> The adult, by the mere fact of being such, generally has the strange illusion that he has now reached his goal; he is pleased with himself, and it does not occur to him that just when he finishes school he should begin to learn in the widest and true *school of life*: he should "take himself in hand" and begin to educate himself. (V. page 29).[162]

In other words, education should be continuous and lifelong — and this is itself a valuable teaching, not to be forgotten. To all, in different ages of life, Assagioli addresses this invitation:

> Keep the fragrance, the best of all ages: the cheerfulness, purity, and simplicity of childhood; the fire of youth; the efficiency and vigor of maturity; the experience, wisdom, and detachment of old age: combine them, have them available, alternate them. (E. p. 117).

Despite the weaknesses, shortcomings and gaps that he found daily in men, Assagioli had great faith in them:

> The great harmony of the Celestial Spheres is also in you: Be silent, listen; you will hear it rise softly and powerfully from the mysterious depths of your being (text written for his son Ilario's book *From Pain to Peace*).

---

[161] *Archive Doc. #11904.* —Ed.

[162] *from "Smiling Wisdom," op.cit.* —Ed.

This operation of trust and esteem must begin in childhood: in him the adult must learn to recognize the potentials that are waiting to manifest themselves in the best way:

In the child "behind" the child, there is a soul, a creature of God who waits to express himself through the little personality (the mask) that is forming. (E. p. 86).

Consequently, the utmost respect for the little ones, for their soul and their spiritual center is needed:

Children are not our creations, they are not soft wax to be molded as we please. They are sacred deposits entrusted by God. (E. p. 86).

And still in the same text we find this confidence expressed both for the child and the adult:

All children have latent "gifts" that can be evoked and valued. We are "super-gifted" in potential and can become so in action, in manifestation.

In this regard, we recall the parable of the three stonecutters, which is very effective in helping us to understand that each activity has its own intrinsic dignity, and that everything depends on the way it is carried out: man can fully express his talents in whatever place in the world that destiny has reserved for him.
The files in the archive are extraordinary containers of wisdom: in the belief that they will in the future be published by the Institute of Psychosynthesis, I quote some passages that I could describe as "pills" of serenity, common sense, kindness, and faith.

The ball falling on the ground immediately rises again: adversity does not last long for the wise (Indian saying).
Balance between old and new: no attachment to the old, and open-mindedness to the new — and absence of the desire for destruction — and to consider the new as the first, raw attempt; an experiment subject to revision, change, improvement (like the history of the car). This requires wisdom.

And here are words to be read with respect, without too many comments: they certainly constituted the basic rationale for Roberto Assagioli's whole life. A title and a brief presentation:

> Make all life sacred.
> Sacrifice = "con-secration," that is, to make sacred what is not, offering it, using it for service, making it available to the Spirit.
> This is true transmutation and sublimation.

Other profound words to give meaning and value to each day of daily life: the leaflet bears a title, *What is Expected*:

> Always be waiting for the great inner event, the illumination, the revelation, the "contact." Wait for the event every morning. Aspire. "Listen."

And in another file from the archive:

> Insist on the great benefits of discovering the value of free things: this discovery gives joy, it gives a sense of inner wealth.

Assagioli does not explain what these "free things" are, but we can imagine that he includes the enjoyment of the beauties of nature, the pleasure of company, the serene evaluation of what one has, good music, good readings. About the books we read for example:

> For a few lire we come into possession of priceless treasures of wisdom, spirituality, experience and beauty.

And with reference to music, Assagioli points out, again in the notes in the archive, that unfortunately today's life does not make sufficient use of this powerful and fascinating medium. We do not know when Assagioli wrote his notes, because the sheets are not dated; however it can be said that he was a precursor of music therapy: the hints of this type of treatment are frequent.[163] Here are some examples:

---

[163] *Assagioli wrote an article titled "Music as a Cause of Disease and as a Healing Agent. (This study was first published in the International Review of Educative Cinematography 5 (1933) 583-595, and was revised and enlarged in 1956, and republished by the Psychosynthesis Research Foundation as its PRF Issue No. 5. —Ed.*

In modern prosaic, practical life, feelings are repressed. Music frees us.

Then an extraordinarily true phrase:

Modern life lacks rhythm ...

And again:

Music has immense power to heal, comfort, cheer —
to restore light, and provide relief to great human pain.
Music has immense power. It is time to use it for the good of humanity, to console, to cheer, to heal souls and bodies.

And finally:

Illnesses for which music therapy can be applied: insomnia, excitement, depression — during childbirth.

Assagioli was really great, at least in my opinion, in his ability to show the hidden value of things that at first glance have none, or very little. And if you follow his reasoning, you always end up agreeing with him. As an example, I quote a passage, also taken from the Archive, in which he expresses acceptance and positive evaluation of an initiative that certainly very few were able to appreciate: the registration required of Jews (il tesseramento). It was during the war, and even with this heavy limitation, which caused so many inconveniences, Assagioli managed to see the beneficial aspects:

Spiritual meaning of the registration.
1) Call for appreciation, for the value of all God's goods.
2) Lessons of detachment, of sobriety, of healthy asceticism.
3) A distinction in practice between the truly necessary and the superfluous.
4) Equality in the face of general needs — team spirit — group organization.
   Don't believe that what we like is a right.
   A perverse tendency not to appreciate what one has or which is abundant.
   Enjoy with gratitude the little we have and we will have. The spiritual attitude of gratitude and appreciation must be taken and maintained towards everything. It actually means recognizing and honoring the presence of

God in all things.
But . . . appreciation, not attachment. This is facilitated precisely by appreciating everything, and not just one special thing.

The words that Assagioli was able to write about the prison experience, reported in the biographical part of this book, come back to mind: even in that circumstance, which few would have been able to evaluate positively, he knew how to find serene words of acceptance and even of appreciation.

We leave the archive and go back for a moment to Ilario's book, *From Pain to Joy*, in which Assagioli's hopelessly ill son collected so many noble and spiritual quotes that had done him good, and seemed worthy of being brought to the attention of other people. Among these quotes, some are from his father, and here we report one that has goodness as its theme:

Let us discover the glories and the power of goodness. Goodness is the opposite of separateness. Goodness smooths what is hard, reconciles opposing beings, brings together what is lost, heals wounds, soothes excited souls, breaks with its subtle and irresistible power the sad, vicious cycles of grudges, envy, jealousies, and hatreds. Goodness is the necessary precursor of Peace. Without goodness there can be no peace, there can be no joy, there can be no love. Goodness is the necessary condition for the righteous and harmonious work of the other "virtues," it is the thread that keeps them united and in agreement with each other and with God.

In addition to goodness, Assagioli urged us to exercise good will — and the subject of will is a theme that we will return to later, a fundamental theme in Assagioli's psychology. Here only one reference is enough, also taken from Ilario's book:

Good will is irresistible. It is a subtle, silent power, which nothing can oppose, to which everything surrenders. Good will unties every knot, escapes every shadow, solves every problem.

Good humor, goodness, goodwill: with these ingredients you can make your life something that has value and meaning. The important thing, says Assagioli, is to never stop, never consider yourself to have "arrived:"

Life is a real school of "initiation." All facts and every external or internal event are exercises, or tasks, or trials (tests), or examinations. (E. p. 117).

And finally two more parables, to illustrate the value of two conditions that seemed essential to Assagioli: harmony and the sense of the relativity of all that is.

In his notes Roberto Assagioli often added images that struck him, passages taken from books he loved, or thoughts of personalities he admired. In the archive, in the file dedicated to C.G. Jung, a scholar with whom Assagioli felt in great harmony and with whom he had had very cordial personal relations, we find a very significant story from the perspective of the great discourse of harmony and the right place in the universe.

The title is *The Rainmaker* (*Il mago della pioggia*, or *The Rain Wizard*). From what can be deduced from the meager comments that appear in the leaflet, it is a personal experience of the famous sinologist Richard Wilhelm[164] who had told it to Jung, who in turn had passed it on to Assagioli during one of their conversations. The story had greatly affected the father of psychosynthesis, so much so that he had transcribed it in a sheet that has been preserved. Here it is:

> In one region of China there had been no rain. A famous rainmaker was called in . . . He came and asked for a secluded cabin. After three days: heavy snowfall. To Wilhelm, who asked him how he did it, he said, "I don't make it rain. In the country where I live, heaven and earth are in harmony and it rains. When I arrived here, I found great separation between heaven and earth, the harmony was broken and this affected me. It took me three days to find harmony, to reunite Heaven and Earth, to be in the Tao!"

A great lesson for today's man, who has lost the sense of belonging to the world in which he lives and has broken the harmony with nature. In his discreet and indirect way, Assagioli manages to say the right things, what we need.

And with reference to the need to realize the relativity of all things, which can have different effects or even contrary to what might appear, in the essay "Cheerfulness" Assagioli cites a Chinese parable taken from the book *The Importance of Living* by Lin Yu Tang:

---

[164] C. G. Jung collaborated a lot with Richard Wilhelm. Wilhelm is responsible for a translation of the famous *I Ching*, the Chinese *Book of Changes*, which in the German and English editions is accompanied by a large preface by Jung himself.

One day an old peasant living with his son on the top of a hill lost his horse. His neighbors sympathized with him over his unfortunate event, but he replied: "How can you tell if it is a misfortune?" Some days later his horse returned leading a number of other horses. The neighbors now wanted to congratulate him on this stroke of good fortune. Also this time the old man replied: "How can you tell if it is a stroke of luck?" The son started to ride these horses and one day broke a leg. The old man's response to his neighbors condolence this time was: "How do you know it is a misfortune?" A little later war broke out, and the son, being disabled, avoided having to take part in it.

Let us always bear this relativity in mind. [165]

The apostle of smiling wisdom knew that living in the right way is also important, above all in view of death and the "hereafter:" a "hereafter" in which he believed with absolute confidence. To conclude this chapter, therefore, I share a very beautiful and profound passage from the Archive in which Assagioli clearly expresses his convictions towards the great appointment that awaits us all:

Death must be overcome — not death, but the terror of death that comes from not understanding life. If you can understand life and its indispensable and beneficial end — death — you will cease to fear it, you will cease to serve your mortal self and serve the immortal: serve God, from whom you come, and to whom you return.[166]

From a spiritual point of view, death does not exist. When we leave the physical body, we move to a more beautiful, brighter and freer life.[167]

The body is a clothing...[168]

---

[165] *This translation is from Psychosynthesis Research Foundation PRF Issue No. 33.* —Ed.
[166] *Archive Doc. #16689.* —Ed.
[167] *Archive Doc. #16698.* —Ed.
[168] *Archive Doc. #16692.* —Ed.

CHAPTER 6
Roberto Assagioli and Borderline Issues

As we have seen, throughout his life Roberto Assagioli was involved with Madame Blavatsky's theosophy, Alice Bailey's Arcane School," and Eastern philosophies; he practiced meditation regularly and was well acquainted with astrology. He was also interested in mediumship and in his younger years, together with Giovanni Papini, scheduled sessions with the famous medium Eusapia Palladino. During his Roman years he joined SIM, the Italian Society of Metapsychics, founded in 1937 and recognized by Royal Decree in 1942, and maintained his membership even after returning to Florence. SIM was not so much concerned with spiritualism, which was all the rage when it was founded, but rather with "psychophysical phenomena," or parapsychology. In Florence, among the lectures he regularly offered to the public, Assagioli also gave some on parapsychological topics. He participated in various conferences on metapsychics, and the Florentine SIM office was based in his home on Via San Domenico. In addition to lectures, Assagioli organized experiments in telepathy, psychometry and precognition with Rhine cards.

Of particular interest was Assagioli's relationship with the Florence 77 Circle and the Florentine medium Roberto Setti (1930-1984). In trance Setti conveyed contents of high ethical and spiritual value that Assagioli had occasion to read. He found them worthy of the greatest attention and wished to meet the young medium. The meeting was very cordial and led to the organization of some private experiments in Assagioli's home. It is also rumored that after the death of his son Ilario, the Assagioli's, particularly his wife, attended Roberto Setti's sessions, but there is no certainty on this point.

The father of psychosynthesis was thus very interested in "borderline issues," which in his opinion demonstrated "the independence of the psyche from the physical body, contributing to the almost certain demonstration of the survival after the death of the physical body." [169]

---

[169] For a more in-depth discussion of these issues, see Francesco Baroni's extensively documented essay "Roberto Assagioli and Parapsychology" in No. 1 of 2024 *Light and Shadow* magazine. *Also see Kenneth Sörensen's e-book compilation* Psychosynthesis and Parapsychology *(2021) available at* https://kennethsorensen.dk/en/product/psychosynthesis-and-parapsychology/. —Ed.

CHAPTER 7
Biopsychosynthesis

Man's energies are many and valuable, that make him strong, healthy, efficient, that give him joys and satisfactions, and that make him an instrument of good for others, and yet he has only a little poor knowledge of how to profit from his riches.
—*R. Assagioli: Psychology and the Art of Living*[170]

In the interview with Sam Keen mentioned earlier, Assagioli clearly stated a few months before he died that "the limitation of psychosynthesis is that it has no limits," and one can only agree with this. We have also seen that, in addition to developing his own movement of psychology and thought, Assagioli contributed to the evolution of psychosomatic medicine, and to humanistic and transpersonal psychology. The discourse is therefore very vast. All that can be done is to say some fundamental things that invite the reader who wishes to learn to go directly to many of Assagioli's texts: in addition to the books, there is a rich collection of articles, essays, and handouts that are available at the Institute of Psychosynthesis in Florence. [171]

We will start from a sacrosanct observation by Roberto Assagioli.

> There is a fundamental deficiency and disproportion in our civilization. Modern man knows many things, he knows how to make admirable use of natural forces, but he generally does not care to explore the *world within him,* to conquer that which constitutes his most intimate and vital part: his *own soul.*[172]

To remedy this serious deficiency, Assagioli developed a very broad and precise conception of the psyche, a real cartography: the famous egg diagram, which has already been presented in the second chapter, and which we present again for clarity of exposure in more detail:

---

[170] Published by the Psychosynthesis Institute of Florence.

[171] Many articles written in Italian are now translated and available at https://kennethsorensen.dk/en/. —Ed.

[172] *from* Psychology and the Art of Living, *page 3.—Ed.*

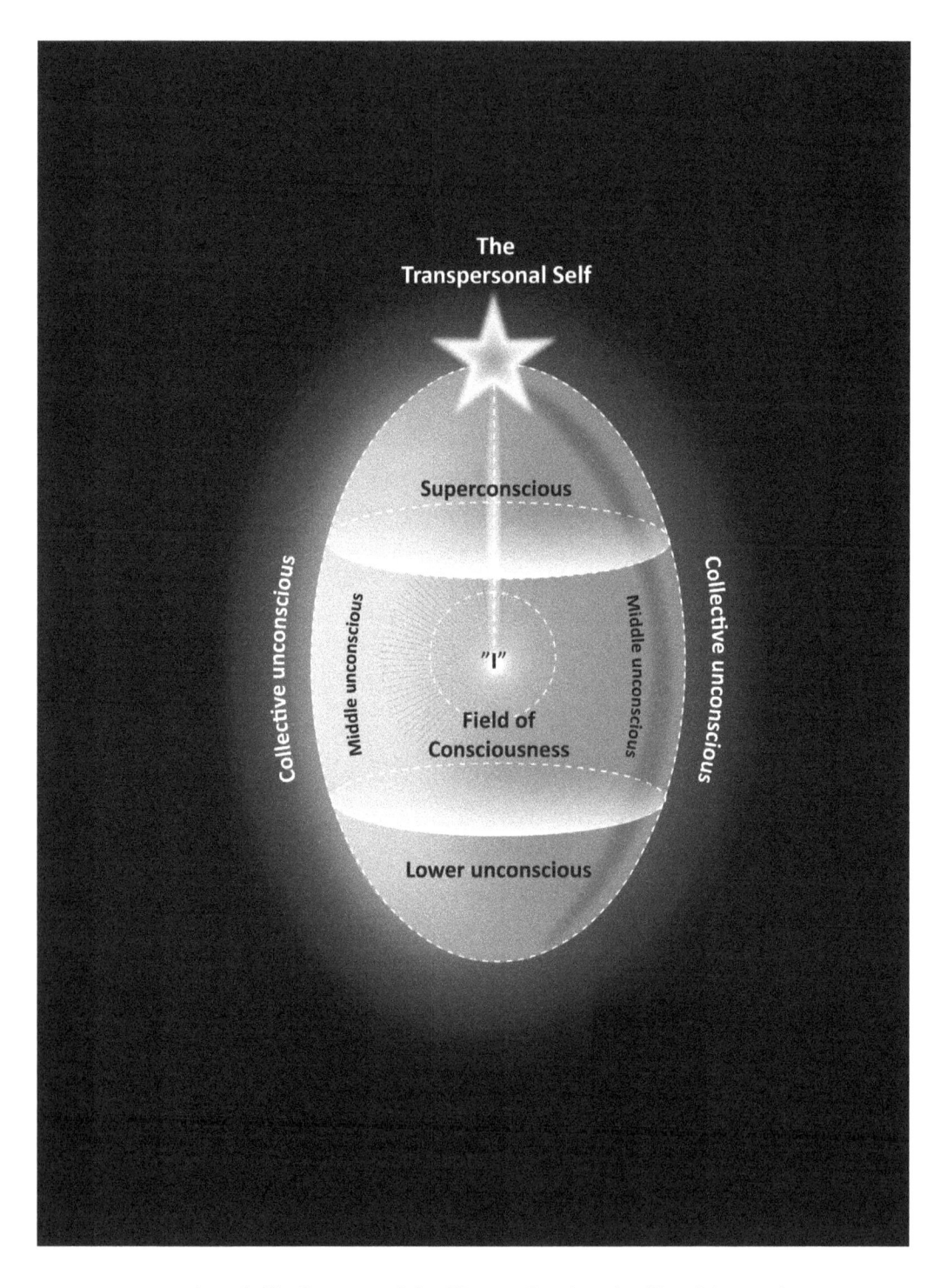

Assagioli's Concept of the Human Psyche: the 'Egg Diagram'

The lower unconscious and the middle unconscious (biological impulses, emotions, latent aspects of the personality, etc.) were the subject of Sigmund Freud's studies and discoveries; the investigation of the upper area (superconscious, or transpersonal unconscious), to which Jung had also dedicated himself, is the most authentically original contribution of Roberto Assagioli. The transpersonal unconscious is the seat of the highest activities (creativity, artistic inspiration, ethical sense, intuition, mystical experiences, etc.) and Assagioli devoted a great deal of attention to this "height psychology," although the object of his psychology is the whole man — body, psyche and spirit. Hence the term *bio-psychosynthesis*, even if the prefix *bio* is generally omitted for brevity.

Consequently, psychosynthetic therapy involves a psychoanalytic phase to ascertain and solve the problems linked to what Freud himself defined as "the cellar," and then to provide support through other techniques — which can be very different depending on the person — to develop, harmonize and integrate all one's tendencies, energies, potentials, higher inclination. This leads to "the penthouse," from which, as Assagioli said, it is possible to admire the starry sky. We also approach the religious sphere, although Assagioli specified that psychosynthesis is "a scientific conception, and as such is neutral towards the various religious forms and the various philosophical doctrines."[173]

Psychosynthesis, in other words, leads "to the threshold of the mystery," and stops there. We know that Assagioli personally went much further, but we also know that he was very keen to keep the two separate and to be very precise and scientific when it came to his psychosynthesis.

One of the strengths of psychosynthesis is the "rediscovery of values." Dr. Vincenzo Liguori, who directed the Psychosynthesis Center in Milan, expresses it very well: "When I approached psychosynthesis through Sergio Bartoli, I came from experiences that led me to use psychology in a very technical way, without too much participation, love, or joy. In psychosynthesis things are very different, and these values are given a lot of importance. I also greatly appreciate Dr. Assagioli's invitation for man to become autonomous and independent, to discover his two poles: his individuality and his universality. And this is vital, especially today when people are undergoing a process of "massification." They develop a mass identity, from which it is good that they emerge to act and move independently, in the awareness of being part of a universal whole."[174]

---

[173] from the article "Psychosynthesis," in *Psychotherapy*, January-March 1976, vol. I, no. 1.

[174] From an interview with the author.

As has already been pointed out, psychosynthesis is therefore above all a psychology for the healthy man, a psychology of health, and is aimed at promoting the harmonious growth and evolution of the individual. To put it in the words of Ms. Maria Luisa Girelli Macchia, former director of the Psychosynthesis Center in Rome and a great connoisseur of Assagioli's work, it tends to

> develop the highest human consciousness, bringing it forth from the tangles, removing everything that covers it and highlighting the diamond that is in each of us. Of course, this is done with respect for each person's timeline, without haste. Assagioli says, however, that once a certain path has been undertaken (and by this he meant in particular the second level of psychosynthesis, that is, transpersonal psychosynthesis), there is no going back.[175]

In this process the role of the therapist is twofold: maternal and paternal. Assagioli explains this clearly in an interview with Stuart Miller in October 1972.[176] The maternal role is suitable for the first part of the treatment and "it consists in giving a sense of protection, understanding, sympathy and encouragement. What a wise mother does." The paternal role, on the other hand, is "training for independence." It consists in developing inner energies and awakening the will. A will intended not in a authoritarian, victorious sense, but as an energy that directs all psychic functions and guides awareness.

With reference to the "egg diagram," it is appropriate to understand well what Assagioli means by the concepts of personal self (or "I") and transpersonal Self. The first, located in the center of the field of consciousness, receives stimuli and contents from the lower, middle and upper unconscious. It is important, says Assagioli, not to identify with them: we have sensations, emotions, thoughts, imaginations, feelings, but we must learn to disidentify ourselves.[177] In fact our

---

[175] From an interview with the author.

[176] Published by the Centro Studi di Psicosintesi «R. Assagioli», piazza Madonna 7, 50123 Florence: Interviews 1972-74. *This quotation is taken from the original interview in English which appeared in* Intellectual Digest, *October 1972. —Ed.*

[177] The exercise of disidentification and self-identification is one of the most important of psychosynthesis. We present it briefly. We generally identify ourselves with our body, with our emotions, with our feelings and with our mind. But it is not so: these are in fact only the instruments of our true self, which is pure consciousness and will. We must learn to take note of this, in order to manage our psychic activities. The exercise, in summary, consists in affirming with conviction and in becoming aware of the fact: "I have a body, but *I am not* my body." Then we move on to the next statement: "I have an emotional life, but *I am not* my emotions, my feelings." And next; "I have a mind, but *I am not* my mind." Indeed body, feelings, minds are changeable and impermanent instruments of experience, perception, action. These statements constitute the preliminary phase of the experience of *self-awareness*: "I am a center of pure awareness, of pure *self-awareness*; I am a center of will, capable of dominating and directing my psychic functions and my body. *I am.*" Daily repetition of this exercise confers security and awareness.

ego, our sense of identity, remains itself although the body changes, and so do the feelings and so on.

In parallel, at a higher level, there is the transpersonal Self, an entity that presides over the higher functions: creativity, intuition, artistic inspiration, moral sense and so on. This is our true center, says Assagioli, of which the "I", or personal self, is a reflection. Generally we are not aware of the transpersonal Self, but we can become so. The identity crises of today's man, who continues to ignore his own being, can be resolved through the development of awareness of the personal self, free from any identification, and the intuition of the transpersonal Self.

Assagioli spoke of personal psychosynthesis and transpersonal psychosynthesis: the first is aimed at the harmonious development and integration of all aspects of the personality — and for many people, Assagioli said, this is enough. For those who feel the yearning for a further expansion of consciousness up to full and authentic self-realization and experience of the Self, there is transpersonal psychosynthesis.

Instead of the term "transpersonal," one could use that of "spiritual." Assagioli however believed that the first expression was more neutral and scientific.

Answering a question from Stuart Miller, who interviewed him again in August 1973,[178] Assagioli explained very clearly what the self-awareness process in psychosynthesis consists of:

> First, preliminary work of personal psychosynthesis, including psychoanalytic phase, though not necessarily a formal, detailed psychoanalysis. After that, and sometimes also concurrently, comes experience of *Self*-awareness. Then, the Self can be called on to guide the whole long process of human development. . . the cultivation of Self-awareness on a wide basis will serve to bring into human life the highest human energies and inspirations. And we sorely need to tap these sources.

In Assagioli's opinion, and also that of C.G. Jung, many crises — especially those of adults — are due precisely to the lack of realization at this level.

To Assagioli, a perfect example of personal and transpersonal psychosynthesis seemed to be represented by the great German poet Johann W. Goethe, who in his long and very active life had gone through different phases: from the *Sturm*

---

[178] This interview was also published in the essay *Interviews* 1972-74, op. cit. *This quotation is taken from the original interview in English which appeared in* Intellectual Digest, *August 1973. —Ed.*

und Drang of his youth to the classicism of maturity to the universal genius of old age. Assagioli writes:

> The comparison between the youthful Goethe, who was romantic, unbridled, sentimental and disorderly, and the mature Goethe, who was "human" in the broadest sense of the word, who made a classical harmony out of his impulsiveness, shows how much can be done for one's own unification, and he consciously accomplished it. [179]

Even Dante's Divine Comedy, with its passage of the protagonist-author from Hell to Purgatory and finally to Paradise, appeared to Assagioli a perfect example of personal and transpersonal psychosynthesis.

* * *

A characteristic feature of psychosynthesis is the use of various psychological techniques to achieve certain purposes, all aimed at growth. One of the most important exercises, both from a personal and social point of view, is that of the transmutation and sublimation of bio-psychic energies; in particular of combative, aggressive and sexual energies, into energies opposite to them and aimed at higher purposes: solidarity, constructiveness, love.

This can be achieved by following certain laws of psychodynamics and using the right techniques in order to "put an end to the enormous waste and misuse of incalculable amounts of sexual, emotional and combative energies, and to direct and use those same forces in creative activities."[180]

Meditation is a very effective method to promote the synthesis, or the harmonious development of all our bio-psycho-spiritual components. Guided and directed by the will, the invaluable quality whose full importance Assagioli first highlighted, meditation disciplines the mind and safeguards it from the typical dispersion of our modern life.

Attention to meditation, which must be combined with visualization, shows the influence of Eastern culture [in psychosynthesis]. Assagioli, however, adapted these techniques to our mentality and used typically Western symbols and concepts.

---

[179] From a lecture in 1933 entitled *The Multiple Mind*.

[180] R. Assagioli, "Psychosynthesis," in *Psychotherapy*, op. cit.

Meditation is a complete exercise, as it involves physical relaxation, emotional stillness, mental recollection, and concentration. Assagioli believed that the external world mirrors the internal one, and is its image and symbol; consequently — for the meditations — he suggested themes symbolizing the development of the personality and upward tension.

Two meditations — symbols of psychosynthesis — are that of the rose and that of the mountain. Assagioli advised Westerners to sit [in a chair], rather than cross-legged, and proposed the rose instead of the lotus flower, because it is closer and more familiar to us. The meaning is however the same. Here are the two meditations:

Exercise of the Rose[181]

After a brief relaxation in a sitting position, imagine that you are on a lawn and see a rose bush in the middle of the lawn. The sky is clear and the sun is shining. Focus your attention on a small bud still enclosed in the green sepals, and imagine seeing it slowly open, unfold, to give rise first to a rose bud and finally to a fully blooming rose. It is important to see the successive stages of opening of the petals, and if possible their movement. Finally, imagine smelling the perfume and touching the velvety petals. In the last stage, imagine identifying yourself with the blooming rose and experiencing this sense of inner openness towards the sun and upwards.

The exercise should be repeated several times before it is successful: at the beginning it is normal to lose concentration or not be able to follow all the different stages.

Exercise of The Mountain

Imagine being in an alpine valley and seeing before us a high mountain with a snow-covered peak. We feel urged to go up, we decide to do it and we start. At the beginning we walk along a comfortable mule track that climbs gently in a pine forest. We climb quickly, feeling the soft ground covered by pine needles under our feet. Then the road becomes steeper, narrows, becomes a path. The pine trees thin out, we come to the meadows. We climb the meadows, and little by little stones begin to appear. After the stones the

---

[181] The rose is the symbol of psychosynthesis and represents inner development.

rock. Here we take a breath, refresh ourselves, then proceed to climb the rock. The difficulties begin, we have to use the holds presented by the rock face, be careful where to put our feet, choose the right places. But we do it with joy, we feel that energies are released in us: in fact, in the face of fatigue and even danger, new forces are manifested. We find areas of snow; then the snow covers the whole rock, and finally we reach the top of the mountain. The air is thin, invigorating, and the spectacle before our eyes is wide and magnificent: above, the immense blue sky and the shining sun. A sense of admiration and joy pervades us.

This exercise of visualization, or rather of imaginative action, is very useful for doing the corresponding exercise of internal ascent. There is in fact a substantial analogy between them: even our "I," our "center of consciousness," can rise along the various levels and aspects of the external world (physical-instinctive-emotional-imaginative-mental-intuitive) up to the luminous peak of spiritual consciousness, of the Self.[182]

These and other exercises are taught during [psychosynthesis] courses and participants are invited to repeat them at home. Work at home, both for patients and for people interested in their inner growth, is very important in psychosynthesis. It involves free drawing, listening to music chosen case by case, repetition of techniques, and exercises of concentration, visualization, meditation, and relaxation. It is also suggested to keep a personal psychological diary, to record dreams, and to read the biographies of outstanding people for inspiration.

* * *

Assagioli, as we have seen, was a pioneer in many fields: he was the first representative in Italy of Freudian psychoanalysis, from which he soon broke away to take his own path. He contributed to the evolution of psychosomatic medicine and already in the 1920-30s he spoke of music therapy and color therapy. He was an initiator of humanistic-existential psychology, in the sense that since the first decades of the century he spoke of a psychology of health; that is, he saw man not only as a bearer of conflict and complexes, but also in his healthier potential and in his need for normality. And finally he was a pioneer of transpersonal psychology,

---

[182] *There are several versions of these exercises in existence, and the source of these versions is not known.* —Ed.

which developed in the 1970s. This considers the states of consciousness that go beyond the ego and that concern "spiritual" experiences, the states of consciousness in which man loses space-time boundaries and enters religious, aesthetic, intuitive dimensions that are fundamental for the development of the personality and whose importance cannot be ignored.

Dr. Laura Boggio Gilot, psychologist, founder and director of the Center for Transpersonal Psychology in Rome, expressed herself in this way about this aspect of Roberto Assagioli's thought:

> Assagioli's model of man, echoed in transpersonal psychology, is a model that includes body, mind and spirit and focuses on the recognition of a spiritual nature that transcends the human being; therefore our potentials are not only potentialities of the psyche, but concern the transcendent, eternal nature. In this sense, therefore, Assagioli recovers an initiatory-spiritual tradition and merges it with psychology. Transpersonal psychology developed Assagioli's discourse on transpersonal development: he said that there are potentials of the higher unconscious, that there is a development beyond the "I" or self, and that this development does not mature in ordinary states of consciousness, but is associated precisely with the transpersonal, with non-ordinary states of consciousness. We are studying the process; that is, we are trying to understand how to access the sublime peaks of the Self, of the spirit, is achieved . . .[183]

All the aspects indicated so far, from the personal to the transpersonal, fall within Assagioli's psychosynthesis, which is very vast and in which the synthesis is intended in an almost alchemical sense, such as sublimation, transformation, harmonization.

It should be emphasized once again that Assagioli was concerned not only with therapy, but the totality of the person; consequently, he tried to promote the development of healthy potentials by every means. In psychosynthesis there is the therapeutic aspect, but also the formative one; it therefore finds application in the educational, social, psychological and mental hygiene fields, and in couples, interpersonal and group relationships as well as in actual therapy.

As has already been pointed out, Assagioli wanted to improve the individual, to work through the individual to transform society and the world in which we

---

[183] From an interview with the author.

live. An interview with Claude Servan Schreiber in 1974 on the theme "Psychology of Women and Couple Relationships"[184] best expresses this. After analyzing the different roles and expounding the criteria that should shape the relationships between men and women ("collaboration and integration on the base of equality"), Assagioli broadens the horizon and outlines his ideal of a society of the future: words that lend themselves well to concluding this brief introduction to his psychosynthesis.

> We know that historically there were matriarchal civilizations and patriarchal civilizations; the ideal would be a new synthetic civilization, that is neither patriarchal nor matriarchal, but one that is psychosynthetic, that is to say, a civilization in which the highest and best qualities of each are manifested.
>
> This would be something new. In all historical civilizations and cultures there has been a preponderance of one or the other element. But in this new civilization and the emerging global culture, for the first time humanity is sufficiently developed to make a planetary, global pattern, incorporating the very best of all men and women. I think that this planetary psychosynthesis, this psychosynthesis of humanity is possible and needed. Each particular problem will then have its frame of reference in the greater whole, and conflict can be replaced by harmonious integration and cooperation. All of this is within our reach — for not only is it very beautiful — it is very human."

---

[184] Published in *Interviews 1972-74*, op. cit. *These quotations are taken from the original interview in English, titled "A Higher View of the Man-Woman Problem," which appeared in the journal* Synthesis, 1, 1, pages 116-123. 1974, 1977. —Ed.

Appendix

INSTITUTE OF PSYCHOSYNTHESIS
Via San Domenico, 16
50133 FLORENCE
Founder: Dr. Roberto Assagioli

Established as a non-profit organization by Decree 1721 of August 1, 1965

MEDITATION AND CONTEMPLATION
Roberto Assagioli

Unrevised Notes from
a Course on Meditation and Contemplation in 1931
(*Document #23630, Assagioli Archives - Florence*) [185]

At the last meeting we talked about meditation, and saw how a complete meditation exercise involves the use of all our normal inner faculties. In fact, meditation requires the successive and simultaneous use of:

1. Memory; 2. Thought; 3. Imagination; 4. Feeling;
5. Desire; 6. Will; Purpose.

The cycle is completed with action.

But there is another inner exercise by which higher levels of consciousness are reached, deeper and more valuable energies are aroused, and more powerful results are achieved, as much in inner transformation as in efficiency and radiance in life. This inner exercise is *contemplation*. Since, however, this word has been

---

[185] *Roberto Assagioli also approached this subject more extensively in a longer essay titled "Contemplation and Illumination" which has been translated into English and is available online at* https://kennethsorensen.dk/en/contemplation-and-illumination/. —Ed.

given different meanings, it is good to specify *how* we understand it, even though it is something that can hardly be expressed in words.

When in the practice of meditation we have reached the highest and most vital point, that is, to arouse the feelings inherent in the theme of meditation, we can pause and rise even higher. With a surge of aspiration, we can almost try to get out of ourselves, to contemplate fixedly the chosen object until we come to empathize and become one with it. This implies a *silence* of all faculties; a special state that is intense concentration on the one hand, and on the other, complete receptivity to the thing contemplated. In this state we forget ourselves; or more precisely, we forget our ordinary personality with its usual states of consciousness (memories, thoughts, images, feelings). But this does not mean that we become unconscious and lazily passive; on the contrary, we are extremely alert; but in a quite different, more subtle, more vibrant sphere of consciousness and inner life.

One has simultaneously a sense of stillness, of perfect peace, and a sense of intense workings taking place spontaneously within us. Because of the first character, it has been called "quiet prayer" by the mystics. They also call contemplation — to use the words of St. Francis de Sales — "a simple and permanent loving attention" of the Spirit (we would say "consciousness") to divine things.[186] And the one who works in us in this state of stillness, in this silence is the superconscious, the Spirit. St. John of the Cross expressed this in a bold but very appropriate and meaningful way, saying that such action is a kind of conception of God in the Soul. In other words, a kind of fertilization of the Soul by the Spirit.

Often, during that silence, there is a vague, indistinct sense of that mysterious work being done at a level that consciousness cannot reach. But the reality of that work is demonstrated by the effects that are seen afterwards. At other times, however, consciousness is able to participate, at least in part, in what is being accomplished in the superconscious: to receive the gifts that descend from Spirit; and then *contemplation* produces *enlightenment*: consciousness finds itself as if bathed in light, and in that light a new faculty of insight, of direct spiritual vision is awakened, by which it discovers new truths, new meanings in the soul and in the universe. Or it realizes the true, profound nature or essence of the thing contemplated, discerns its value, its relationships, its place in the Great Reality. This Light is joined by a sense of expansion, enlargement, joy, peace; of security, of power. It is a true inner transfiguration.

---

[186] (See St. Francis de Sales, *Amour de Dieu* [*Love of God*], VI, Ch. 3; See Lamballe, *La Contemplation* [*Contemplation*]) —Assagioli's original lecture note.

This high state of consciousness lasts for a more or less long time, then it gradually fades away, and to our regret we are forced to descend into the heavy, dense atmosphere of the ordinary levels of daily life. But we are no longer what we were before: a change has taken place; a "sign" has been imprinted in us. We can no longer give so much importance and value to the things of ordinary life; ordinary passions no longer have the power over us that they did before; human attachments have loosened their grip; the ambitions, desires, and goals pursued by ordinary humanity no longer fascinate or exalt us. We have glimpsed another reality that is wider and higher, brighter, *truer*, and we feel a subtle longing, a pressing call, an irrepressible aspiration toward that spiritual sphere. But this does not make us passive dreamers. New goals and new work for good excite us, new inner achievements attract us, and we return with increased fervor, with firmer faith, and with firmer purpose, to *act*.

This vision of the admirable possibilities, of the precious fruits of meditation and contemplation, prompts us to take a more lively and conscious interest in the ways of practicing them. What is important is the choice of the object, the theme to be proposed. Such objects are quite diverse and their choice depends:

(a) On the end we wish to achieve.
(b) On the particular psychological type to which we belong.

The consideration of the first element is quite easy. For example, if we wish to develop a certain quality or virtue (opposite to a defect we deplore in ourselves), that will naturally form the subject of meditation. Thus we may meditate on calmness, courage, confidence, goodness, generosity, humility, wisdom, energy, love, gladness.

If our aspiration turns to realize spiritual consciousness directly, we will choose the most suitable objects for that, which we will name below.

More difficult, however, is to know which objects and methods are most convenient and bear best fruit in relation to our particular individual constitution. The study of the various psychological types and methods of inner development most suited to each of us is very interesting and can give valuable standards of knowledge and life, but it requires extensive examination. In the meantime, the best method to follow is the experimental one: that is, to *try out* various objects of meditation little by little and thus discover which (or which one) is best suited to our temperament and gives us the best results.[187] Let us now see what these themes are to choose from.

---

[187] *The author's revised text stopped here; however we include Archive Document #23630 in its entirety, which includes the section on Meditation Themes which follows.* —Ed.

MEDITATION THEMES

1. A phrase, a motto, a thought. A verse that we like and that fits.

2. An abstract idea, a universal principle.

3. A broader theme that lends itself to the unfolding of thoughts to the evocation of feelings. *Meditations on nature.* (Anile, Michelet, Febre) *Geological* (De Lorenzo) - *Astronomical* (Flammarion). [188]

4. Imaginative evocation of concrete scenes apt to shake, arouse: Meditation on the *Passion*, much used by those who are religious. The exercises of St. Ignatius.[189]

5. An inherent quality, a virtue, a spiritual note.

6. One's Self endowed that quality or virtue.

7. An embodied ideal, a Great Being (e.g. the Christ).

8. The spiritual Self, the true I, as the Center of Reality, of Life, of Light.

9. The perfected Self.

10. The Light of the Spirit (Patanjali, I, 36). [190]

11. Union with all beings. Spiritual Love. Sense of the unity of Life.

---

[188] *In Assagioli Archive Doc.#11790 there is a hand-written note concerning nature symbols that explicitly refers to Antonio Salvatore Anile (1869-1943), Jules Michelet (1798-1874), Maurice Maeterlinck (1862-1949), and Jean-Henri Fabre (1823-1915). La Grande Féerie was one of the works of Maeterlinck. Giuseppe De Lorenzo (1971-1957), was professor of geology at the University of Naples and author of numerous works. Nicolas Camille Flammarion (1842-1925), was a French astronomer and author of numerous works and publisher of the magazine L'Astonomie. —Ed.*

[189] *During the 1520's, St. Ignatius Loyola began writing about the emotions that took hold of him — feelings of gratitude and anguish, consolation and sadness — while encountering the Scriptures. Those meditations eventually became the Spiritual Exercises, which were first published in 1548. The Spiritual Exercises is a compilation of meditations, prayers, and other contemplative practices. It is not like other classics in Western spirituality that are typically read from beginning to end. It is more like a handbook, especially for use by spiritual directors who accompany and guide people through this dynamic process of reflection.—Ed.*

[190] *Patanjali, Yoga Sutras, I.36: "Through meditation on the Light one can attain knowledge of the Spirit."—Ed.*

12. A significant symbol.
    (a) The Cross
    (b) The Jewel in the lotus
    (c) The Grail[191]
    THE GRAIL: (merits - suggestive, universal):
        The Grail cup = Center of individuality.
        The Grail temple = The personality.
        Surrounding landscape = Field of work.
        Scene of the Descent of the Grail.

---

[191] *The Grail (Graal in Italian and old French, often referred to as The Holy Grail) is at the center of a group of spiritual stories and legends, the earliest known written version is by Wolfram von Eschenbach about 1217, based upon a French romance. Titurel and Parsifal are knights of the Grail. In his essay on "Contemplation and Illumination," Assagioli says, "Each of us must relive in himself the story of Titurel, the first knight of the Grail, in all its significant details."*—Ed.

The Assagioli Archive
Sergio Guarino

The manuscript of "Meditation and Contemplation" was taken from the Assagioli Archive *(Document #23630)*. The work of reorganizing and cataloging Roberto Assagioli's written material, including many autographs, is the continuation of what was begun in 1974 by Piero Ferrucci. He created the current Assagioli Archive, which is preserved in Roberto Assagioli's Studio on the first floor of the *Istituto di Psicosintesi* headquarters in Florence, which still attracts visitors and researchers, even from abroad.

This is a considerable heritage of notes, reflections, and international correspondence, which testifies to the vastness of the relationships and the breadth of the interests of the founder of psychosynthesis. The writings are in various languages, and range from small hand-written notes on the most disparate themes of the growth of the human soul, to complete texts, many of which are unpublished.

The archiving work has required the careful examination and cataloguing of each element to achieve accessibility and usability for those who wish to come into contact with Roberto Assagioli's working methods and his sources of inspiration.

The Assagioli Archive is online at www.archivioassagioli.org, where images of thousands of manuscripts and documents left by Roberto Assagioli and preserved at the headquarters of the Institute of Psychosynthesis, at Via San Domenico 16 in Florence, can be viewed. This is an ongoing activity of great interest for psychosynthesis practitioners and others, which makes new material available for consultation.

By 2023, the approximately 19,000 documents of the Studio Archive with manuscript notes already available online were augmented by those preserved in another section of the archive, the Synthesis File. These are the printed publications of Assagioli's writings, the typewritten texts of lessons and conferences, the drafts of articles and books written in Italian and English, but also in many other languages. All the documents, divided by language and ordered alphabetically by title, have been scanned and catalogued to make research and consultation easier. This addition is of great interest for deepening the knowledge of Roberto Assagioli's thought, which covers a very long period of time, from the first writings of 1905 to 1974.

Selected Bibliography

This Bibliography contains references and authors cited in the Italian edition, as well as English translations of the works of those authors. There are now numerous books on Assagioli and psychosynthesis in many languages.

Assagioli, Ilario, *Dal dolore alla pace* [From Pain to Peace], Editrice Nuova Era, Vitinia di Roma, 1972.

—, *Poesie e Diario spirituale* [Poems and Spiritual Diary], Editrice Nuova Era, Vitinia di Roma, 1972.

Assagioli, Roberto, *Psychosynthesis: A Manual of Principles and Techniques,* Hobbs, Dorman & Company, Inc. New York, 1965.

—, *Life as a Game and Stage Performance (Role Playing)* and *Cheerfulness (A Psychosynthetic Technique),* Psychosynthesis Research Foundation PRF Issue No. 33, 1973.

—, *Principi e metodi della psicosintesi terapeutica,* Astrolabio, Roma, 1973.

—, *Psicosintesi, armonia della vita,* Edizioni Mediterranee, Roma, 1971.

—, *The Act of Will,* Viking Press, New York, 1973.

—, *L'atto di volontà,* Astrolabio, Roma, 1973.

—, "The Golden Mean of Roberto Assagioli," Interview with Sam Keen, in *Psychology Today,* December 1974

—, *Per vivere meglio,* Istituto di Psicosintesi, Firenze, 1975.

—, *I tipi umani,* Istituto di Psicosintesi, Firenze, 1976.

—, Psychosynthesis Typology, Institute of Psychosynthesis, London, 1983.

—, *Interviste 1972-74,* Centro Studi di Psicosintesi, "R. Assagioli", Firenze, 1987.

—, *Interviews,* online at https://kennethsorensen.dk/en/?s=Interview&id=10440.

—, *Intervista con Sam Keen,* Centro Studi di Psicosintesi "R. Assagioli", Firenze, 1987.

—, *La psicologia e l'arte di vivere,* Istituto di Psicosintesi, Firenze, 1988.

—, *Lo sviluppo transpersonale,* Astrolabio, Roma, 1988.

—, *Educare l'uomo domani,* Istituto di Psicosintesi, Firenze, 1988.

—, *Comprendere la psicosintesi,* Astrolabio, Roma, 1991.

—, *Transpersonal Development,* Inner Way Productions, Findhorn, Scotland, 2007.

—, *Freedom in Jail,* Florence, Istituto di Psicosintesi, 2016.

—, *Roberto Assagioli in His Own Words: Fragments of an Autobiography,* Florence, stituto di Psicosintesi, 2019.

—, *Creating Harmony in Life: A Psychosynthesis Approach,* Florence, Istituto di Psicosintesi, 2022.
—, *Psychosynthesis of the Couple, edited by Jan Kuniholm.* Cheshire Cat Books, 2022.
Bailey, Alice, *Biografia incompiuta-, Iniziazione umana e solare-, Il disce polato nella Nuova Era, Trattato dei sette raggi* (tutti editi da Casa Editrice Nuova Era, Casalpalocco Roma).
—, *Initiation Human And Solar,* Lucis Press, New York, 1922.
—, *A Treatise on White Magic,* Lucis Press, New York, 1934.
—, *Discipleship in the New Age* (2 Volumes), Lucis Press, New York, 1944.
—, *The Unfinished Autobiography,* Lucis Press, New York, 1951.
Baldini, Anna, *Quaderno di biopsicosintesi,* Istituto di Psicosintesi, Firenze, 1989.
Baroni, Francesco, *Assagioli and Parapsychology,* Luce e Ombra, 2024.
Berti, Alessandro, *Roberto Assagioli. Gli anni della formazione,* Istituto di Psicosintesi, Firenze, 1987.
—, et. al, *Roberto Assagioli 1888-1988,* Centro Studi di Psicosintesi "R. Assagioli," Firenze, 1988.
Bocconi, Andrea, *Psychosynthesis in Education,* Zonafranca Editrice, 2018.
Boggio, Gilot Laura, *Psicosintesi e meditazione,* Edizioni Mediterranee, Roma, 1983.
Caldironi Bruno, *Seminari di psicopatologia e psicoterapia,* Editore C. Nanni, Ravenna, 1992.
—*L'uomo a tre dimensioni,* Edizioni di Girasole, Ravenna, 2004
Ferrucci, Piero, *Crescere: teoria e pratica della psicosintesi,* Astrolabio, Roma, 1981.
—, *What We May Be: Techniques for Psychological and Spiritual Growth Through Psychosynthesis,* Turnstone, London, 1982.
—, *Esperienze delle vette,* Astrolabio, Roma, 1989.
—, *Inevitable Grace: Breakthroughs in the Lives of Great Men and Women: Guides to Your Self-Realization,* J.P. Tarcher, New York, 1990.
—, *Introduzione alla psicosintesi,* Edizioni Mediterranee, Roma, 1994.
—, *What Our Children Teach Us: Lessons in Joy, Love and Awareness,* Grand Central Publishing, 2001.
—, *The Power of Kindness: The Unexpected Benefits of Leading a Compassionate Life,* J.P. Tarcher, New York, 2006.
—, *Beauty and the Soul: The Extraordinary Power of Everyday Beauty to Heal Your Life,* J.P. Tarcher, New York, 2009.
—, *Your Inner Will: Finding Personal Strength in Critical Times,* J.P. Tarcher, New York, 2015.
Freud, Sigmund, *Tre saggi sulla teoria della sessualità.*

—, *Three Essays on the Theory of Sexuality, 1905.*
—, *Analisi dei sogni.*
—, *Interpretation of Dreams*
—, *Complete Psychological Works, Revised Standard Edition,* Rowan & Littlefield, 2024.
Freud-Jung, *Lettere,* Boringhieri, Torino, 1974.
Freud, Sigmund and Jung, C.G. *Letters,* Abridged Edition, Princeton University Press, 1994.
Jung, C.G., *Memories, Dreams, Reflections,* Pantheon Books, 1973.
—, *Collected Works,* Routledge, 1973.
—, *Ricordi, sogni, riflessioni,* BUR, Milano 1984.
Gaddini, Eugenio: *Il movimento psicoanalitico in Italia,* Cortina Editore, Milano, 1989.
Giovetti, Paola, *H.P. Blavatsky e la Società Teosofica,* Edizioni Mediterranee, Roma, 1991.
—, *I grandi Iniziati del nostro tempo,* Rizzoli, Milano, 1993.
Hardy, Jean, *A Psychology with a Soul,* Routledge and Kegan Paul Ltd., London, 1987.
Jones, Ernest, *The Life and Work of Sigmund Freud,* Basic Books, 1960.
—, *Vita e opere di Freud,* Il Saggiatore, Milano, 1962.
Lunelli, Luisa, *Roberto, Nella e Luisa,* Centro Studi di Psicosintesi «R. Assagioli», Firenze, 1991.
—, *Roberto, Nella and Luisa (English translation)* https://kennethsorensen.dk/en/roberto-nella-and-luisa/
Macchia, Marialuisa, *Roberto Assagioli: La Psicosintesi - Il profilo della coscienza di un uomo che ha parlato della vita con l'intelligenza del cuore, come trespare dalla lettura del suo lavoro.* Edizioni Nomina, Rome, 2000.
Marabini, Enrico, *Roberto Assagioli e la biopsicosintesi,* «Luce e Ombra», Bologna, n. 1/1989.
Pellerin, Monique, Brés Micheline, *La Psychosynthèse,* Presse Universitaire de France, Paris, 1994.
Rosselli, Massimo, *I nuovi paradigmi della psicologia,* Cittadella Editrice, Assisi, *1992.*
—, *Introduzione alla psicosintesi,* Istituto di Psicosintesi, Firenze.
Tillì, Sebastiano, *Concetti della psicologia umanistica di Roberto Assagioli,* Istituto di Psicosintesi, Firenze, 1980.
Wehr, Gerhard, *Jung,* Rizzoli, Milano, 1987.
—, *Martin Buber,* Diogenes Verlag, Zürich, 1991.

Psychosynthesis in the World

There are now psychosynthesis centers, teachers, practitioners and opportunities around the world: In Italy, France, Germany, United Kingdom, Ireland, Netherlands, Belgium, Norway, Sweden, Denmark, Finland, Poland, Russia, Czech Republic, Slovakia, Spain, Portugal, Switzerland, Austria, Bosnia and Herzegovina, Serbia, Greece, Bulgaria, Romania, Israel, Jordan, Mexico, Brazil, Argentina, Ecuador, Peru, Chile, Canada, The United States, Japan, Australia, New Zealand, Sri Lanka, India, Pakistan, and other countries, as well an numerous opportunities online. There are professional associations of psychosynthesis therapists and coaches in many countries worldwide.

Printed in the USA
CPSIA information can be obtained
at www.ICGtesting.com
CBHW041544241024
16327CB00041B/980